THE LANGUAGE GYM

THE LANGUAGE GYM

ITALIAN SENTENCE BUILDERS

A lexicogrammar approach

PRIMARY

Copyright © G. Conti and D. Viñales

Imprint: Language Gym

THE LANGUAGE GYM

About the authors

Simona Gravina has taught for 16 years, in schools in Italy and the UK, both in state and independent settings. She lives in Glasgow, Scotland. She is fluent in three languages and gets by in a few more. Simona is, besides a teacher, a mum, a bookworm, a passionate traveller and a fitness enthusiast. In the last three years she has been testing and implementing E.P.I. in one of the top Independent schools in Scotland, St Aloysius' College, where she is currently Modern Languages Curriculum Leader in the Junior School. In addition, Simona is a committee member of SALT, Scottish Association for Languages Teachers.

Stefano Pianigiani is a Language Development Leader, teaching Primary and Secondary pupils at Appleton Academy in Bradford, England. He is an ECT mentor and SCITT MFL tutor for Exceed Academy Trust. He is fluent in four languages, and has taught Spanish, Italian and French all the way from Primary to A Level. He has a wide cultural experience having studied and lived in Italy, Spain and England. Stefano has completed his MA in Education at Leeds Trinity University. He is an enthusiastic educator and fervent creator of resources who has fully embraced Dr Conti's teaching from its very origins.

Francesca Ciaravino has been teaching for 5 years in both private and state settings. She is passionate about travelling and cooking. She fell in love with teaching after her Erasmus experience in France, Tours specifically. After few years she decided to explore England where she decided to settle. Since the pandemic she has been implementing the EPI method in her school where she is currently second in department.

Christian Moretti has been teaching Modern Foreign Languages (Spanish and Italian) for over fifteen years in the UK and Ireland. He has been an Associate for Junior Cycle for Teachers, a Department of Education of Ireland agency and the National Council for Curriculum and Assessment of Ireland. He has been awarded a PhD in Comparative Literature (Spanish and Italian) by the University of Kent (UK). As a scholar, Christian has published numerous research papers in prestigious academic journals in the literary and medical humanities fields. He is currently a teacher of Modern Foreign Languages in Limerick Educate Together Secondary School (Ireland). Christian is passionate about wellbeing and equality, he is a fervent advocate for an inclusive education which is accessible to all. Christian has fully embraced Dr. Conti's research-based language teaching method from the beginning and is a very active resources creator. Christian is fluent in four languages.

Gianfranco Conti taught for 25 years at schools in Italy, the UK and in Kuala Lumpur, Malaysia. He has also been a university lecturer, holds a Master's degree in Applied Linguistics and a PhD in metacognitive strategies as applied to second language writing. He has co-authored the best-selling and influential book for world languages teachers, "The Language Teacher Toolkit", "Breaking the sound barrier: Teaching learners how to listen", in which he puts forth his Listening As Modelling methodology and "Memory: what every language teacher should know". Last but not least, Gianfranco has created the instructional approach known as E.P.I. (Extensive Processing Instruction).

Dylan Viñales has taught for 15 years, in schools in Bath, Beijing and Kuala Lumpur in state, independent and international settings. He lives in Kuala Lumpur. He is fluent in five languages, and gets by in several more. Dylan is, besides a teacher, a professional development provider, specialising in E.P.I., metacognition, teaching languages through music and cognitive science. In the last five years, together with Dr Conti, he has driven the implementation of E.P.I. in one of the top international schools in the world: Garden International School. Dylan authors an influential blog on modern language pedagogy in which he supports the teaching of languages through E.P.I.

DEDICATION

For my daughter Giulia
-Simona

For Skyla & Tessa
-Stefano

For my husband, Luca
-Francesca

For my parents and Gary
-Christian

For Catrina
-Gianfranco

For Ariella & Leonard
-Dylan

Acknowledgements

Creating a book is a time-consuming yet rewarding endeavour.

Simona would like to thank her daughter Giulia, currently a Primary student, for all her encouragement and for actively testing and giving feedback on the tasks. Huge gratitude to her twin Primary teacher Emanuela for feedback on specific tasks. Secondly, she would like to thank at St Aloysius' College, especially Giulia Frisina for all the contributions and advice in testing the tasks as a trained E.P.I. teacher, who has fully implemented Dr. Conti's methodology in the classroom.

Stefano is indebted to his mother Maria who has offered her constant help and support, and to his fiancée Tessa who has helped him in choosing the best Faulty Echo English native speaker misconceptions.

Francesca would like to thank her Head of Faculty, Mrs Yasmine Benderbouz for giving her full support and freedom to experiment with the EPI method within the Spanish Faculty. She would also like to thank the whole Italian Sentence Builder crew for involving her in this amazing project.

Christian is deeply indebted to his parents, Adelaide and Damiano for always supporting him and inspiring him in his teaching career. He is also immensely grateful to all the generations of students he has had the privilege to teach, their feedback, their attention and their enthusiasm. He would also like to thank all those colleagues who have shared his passion for E.P.I. and have supported him over time.

Our sincere gratitude to all the people involved in the recording of the Listening audio files: Francesca Bonsignori, Ivano Confalone, Liliana Falsini, and guest star Dr Gianfranco Conti. Your energy, enthusiasm and passion comes across clearly in every recording and is the reason why the listening sections are such a successful and engaging resource, according to the many students who have been alpha and beta testing the book.

Thanks to Flaticon.com and Mockofun.com for providing access to a limitless library of engaging icons, clipart and images which we have used to make this book more user-friendly than any other Sentence Builders predecessor, with a view to be as engaging as possible for primary level students.

Finally, our gratitude to the MFL Twitterati for their ongoing support of E.P.I. and the Sentence Builders book series. In particular a shoutout to our team of incredible educators who helped in checking all the units: Cristina Mari, Giovanni Calandro, Ambrogio de Santis, Alberta Capasso, Sophie Neil & Regina Vara Corella. It is thanks to your time, patience, professionalism and detailed feedback that we have been able to produce such a refined and highly accurate product.

Grazie a tutti,
Simona, Stefano, Francesca, Christian, Gianfranco & Dylan

Introduction

Hello and welcome to the first Sentence Builders workbook designed for Primary aged children, designed to be an accompaniment to an Italian Extensive Processing Instruction course. The book has come about out of necessity, because such a resource did not previously exist.

How to use this book if you have bought into our E.P.I. approach

This book was originally designed as a resource to use in conjunction with our E.P.I. approach and teaching strategies. Our course favours flooding comprehensible input, organising content by communicative functions and related constructions, and a big focus on reading and listening as modelling. The aim of this book is to empower the beginner learner with linguistic tools - high-frequency structures and vocabulary - useful for real-life communication. Since, in a typical E.P.I. unit of work, aural and oral work play a huge role, this book should not be viewed as the ultimate E.P.I. coursebook, but rather as a **useful resource** to **complement** your Listening-As-Modelling and Speaking activities.

Sentence Builders – Online Versions

Please note that this book is best used in synergy with **language-gym.com** and **sentencebuilders.com**. Both websites feature self-marking games and activities based on its content. The sentence builders will be available in bilingual and Italian only versions on the Language Gym website, available to download, editable and in landscape design optimised for displaying in the classroom, via the Locker Room section. **A subscription is required to access the content on both sites.**

How to use this book if you don't know or have NOT bought into our approach

Alternatively, you may use this book to dip in and out of as a source of printable material for your lessons. Whilst our curriculum is driven by communicative functions rather than topics, we have deliberately embedded the target constructions in topics which are popular with teachers and commonly found in published coursebooks.

If you would like to learn about E.P.I. you could read one of the authors' blogs. The definitive guide is Dr Conti's "Patterns First – How I Teach Lexicogrammar" which can be found on his blog (www.gianfrancoconti.com). There are also blogs on Dylan's wordpress site (mrvinalesmfl.wordpress.com) such as "Using sentence builders to reduce (everyone's) workload and create more fluent linguists" which can be read to get teaching ideas and to learn how to structure a course, through all the stages of E.P.I.

Examples of E.P.I. activities and games to play in class, based on MARS EARS sequence, can be found in Simona's padlet (https://en-gb.padlet.com/simograv/svi55fluxeolisi9) "MFL Teaching based on E.P.I. approach, Videos and blogs, Sample activities from Modelling to Spontaneity". These can be used to model tasks.

The book "Breaking the Sound Barrier: Teaching Learners how to Listen" by Gianfranco Conti and Steve Smith, provides a detailed description of the approach and of the listening and speaking activities you can use in synergy with the present book.

The structure of the book

This book contains 10 units which concern themselves with a specific communicative function, such as 'I can say my name and age', 'I can talk about the weather', 'I can say what's in my town'. You can find a note of each communicative function in the Table of Contents. Each unit includes:

- a sentence builder modelling the target constructions, introduced by questions to guide communication;
- a set of Listening-As-Modelling activities to train decoding skills, sound awareness, speech-segmentation, lexical-retrieval and parsing skills;
- a set of reading tasks focusing on both the meaning and structural levels of the text;
- a set of translation tasks aimed at consolidation through retrieval practice;
- a set of writing tasks targeting essential writing micro-skills such as spelling, functional and positional processing, editing and communication of meaning.

Each sentence builder at the beginning of a unit contains one or more constructions which have been selected with real-life communication in mind. Each unit is built around that construction but not solely on it. Based on the principle that each E.P.I instructional sequence must move from modelling to production in a seamless and organic way, each unit expands on the material in each sentence builder by embedding it in texts and graded tasks which contain both familiar and unfamiliar (but comprehensible and learnable) vocabulary and structures. Through lots of careful recycling and thorough and extensive processing of the input, by the end of each unit the student has many opportunities to encounter and process the new vocabulary and patterns with material from the previous units.

Alongside the units you will find: No Snakes No Ladders tasks created to practise speaking skills with an engaging and fun board game that can be photocopied and played in groups of 3 students.

Important *caveat*

1) This is a '**no frills**' book. This means that there are a limited number of illustrations. This is because we want every single little thing in this book to be useful. We have given serious thought to both **recycling** and **interleaving**, in order to allow for key constructions, words and grammar items to be revisited regularly so as to enhance exponentially their retention.

2) **Listening** as modelling is an essential part of E.P.I. The listening files for each listening unit can be found in the AUDIO section on Language-Gym.com - a subscription to the website is **not required** to access these.

3) **All content** in this booklet matches the content on the **Language Gym** website. For best results, we recommend a mixture of communicative, retrieval practice games, combined with Language Gym games and workouts, and then this booklet as the follow-up, either in class or for homework.

4) This booklet is suitable for **beginner** learners. This equates to a **CEFR A1-A2** level, or a beginner **KS2 (or a less strong KS3)** class. You do not need to start at the beginning, although you may want to dip in to certain units for revision/recycling. You do not need to follow the booklet in order, although many of you will, and if you do, you will benefit from the specific recycling/interleaving strategies. Either way, all topics are repeated frequently throughout the book.

We do hope that you and your students will find this book useful and enjoyable.

Table of Contents

Unit	Topic	Page
1 Mi chiamo	I can say my name & age	1
2 L'alfabeto	Alphabet and phonics / decoding skills	13
3 Come stai?	I can greet and express how I am	19
4 Il mio compleanno	I can say when my birthday is	30
5 Il mio animale domestico	I can say what pets I have	49
6 La mia cartella	I can say what's in my schoolbag	69
7 Di dove sei?	I can talk about countries and languages	91
8 Che tempo fa?	I can talk about the weather	110
9 La mia città	I can talk about where I live	125
10 Nel mio paese	I can say what is in my town	144

UNIT 1
MI CHIAMO

In this unit you will learn how to say in Italian:

- ✓ What your name is
- ✓ How old you are
- ✓ Hello and good morning
- ✓ Numbers 1 to 12

THE LANGUAGE GYM

UNIT 1. MI CHIAMO
I can say my name and age

> **Come ti chiami?** *What's your name?*
> **Quanti anni hai?** *How old are you?*

| Ciao
Hello

Buongiorno
Good
morning

Buon
pomeriggio
Good
afternoon

Buonasera
Good
evening | mi chiamo
my name is | **Alessandro**
Anna
Carlo
Christian
Daniela
Davide
Dylan
Fabio
Francesca
Gianfranco
Gianni
Giulia
Laura
Maria
PierPaolo
Roberto
Simona
Stefano | **e**
and | **ho**
*I have** | **un** *1*

due 2
tre 3
quattro 4
cinque 5
sei 6
sette 7
otto 8
nove 9
dieci 10
undici 11
dodici 12 | **anno**
year

anni
years |

***Author's notes** - In Italian you do not say *I am five years old* but *I have 5 years.*
e.g. *Ho cinque anni*

Unit 1. My name and age: LISTENING

1. Listen and complete with the missing vowel 

a. Mi ch__amo

b. H__ otto anni

c. Ho se__ anni

d. Ho cinqu__ anni

e. Ho und__ci anni

f. Ho nov__ anni

g. Ho d__eci anni

h. Quanti anni h__i?

i. Ho d__dici anni

j. Ho sett__ anni

a	e	i	o	u

2. Break the flow: Draw a line between words 

a. MichiamoAnnaehocinqueanni

b. BuonaseramichiamoCarla

c. CiaomichiamoFilippoehosetteanni

d. BuongiornomichiamoChristianhoseianni

e. Ciaoquantiannihai?Hodiecianni

f. Buongiorno,cometichiami?MichiamoFrancesca

g. Ciaocometichiami?Equantiannihai?

h. BuongiornomichiamoMarcellohonoveanni

3. Listen and tick one option for each sentence 

		1	2	3
a.	Mi chiamo	Giulia	Gianfranco	Gianni
b.	Ho	dodici anni	due anni	quattro anni
c.	Ho	dieci anni	dodici anni	undici anni
d.	Ciao	quanto anni ai?	quanti anno hai?	quanti anni hai?

4. Complete with the missing syllables in the box below

a. Come ti chia _ _ ?

b. Mi _ _ _ _ _ mo Roberto.

c. Ho cin _ _ _ anni.

d. _ _ _ _ _ giorno.

e. Ciao, mi chia_ _ Gianni.

f. _ _ _ _ ti anni hai?

g. _ _ sette anni.

h. Ho dodi _ _ anni.

i. Mi chi_ _ _ Maria.

j. _ _ _ _ _, mi chiamo Simona.

| Quan | Ho | que | amo | Ciao | chia | mi | mo | Buon | ci |

5. Fill in the grid with the correct information 

	Name	Age (Number)
a.		
b.		
c.		
d.		

6. Faulty Echo

e.g. Ciao, ho <u>sei</u> anni.

a. Ho nove anni.

b. Ciao, ho dodici anni

c. Buongiorno, mi chiamo Maria.

d. Ciao, ho undici anni.

e. Ciao, mi chiamo Ilaria e ho dieci anni.

f. Mi chiamo Liliana e ho sette anni.

g. Quanti anni hai?

7. Track the sounds

Listen and write down how many times you will hear the sound

1.	a	
2.	e	
3.	i	
4.	o	
5.	u	

8. Spot the Intruder

Identify and underline the word in each sentence the speaker is NOT saying

e.g. <u>Ciao</u>, mi chiamo Maria.

a. Come ti chiami? Non mi chiamo PierPaolo.

b. Quanti anni hai? Ho dodici undici anni.

c. Buonasera, mi me chiamo Giulia.

d. Ciao Simona, come ti chiami?

e. Ciao, mi chiamo Anna e ho sei sette anni.

f. Buongiorno, mi ti chiamo Antonio e ho cinque anni.

g. Buonasera, mi chiamo Simone e ho hai tredici anni.

9. Spelling Challenge (1-12)
Listen and complete the Spanish words with the missing letter.

a.	D__e	g.	Ot__o
b.	U__o	h.	T__e
c.	S__i	i.	Quat__ro
d.	N__ve	j.	S__tte
e.	C__nque	k.	Dodi__i
f.	Di__ci	l.	Undi__i

10. Listen and circle the correct number (1-12)

e.g. Quanti anni hai? Ho nove anni

e.g.	7	8	9
a.	6	7	8
b.	10	3	2
c.	9	12	11
d.	4	5	1
e.	12	6	4
f.	3	13	10
g.	11	3	13
h.	8	6	7

Unit 1. My name and age: VOCABULARY BUILDING

1. Match Up

1.	Mi chiamo		a.	Ten
2.	Dieci		b.	Four
3.	Tre		c.	Two
4.	Quattro		d.	Five
5.	Due		e.	My name is
6.	Tredici		f.	Seven
7.	Undici		g.	Three
8.	Anni		h.	Thirteen
9.	Cinque		i.	Years
10.	Sette		j.	Eleven

1	
2	
3	
4	
5	
6	
7	
8	
9	
10	

2. Broken Words

a.	H______	*I have*
b.	O______	*Eight*
c.	Se_____	*Six*
d.	A______	*Years*
e.	Mi chi__	*My name is*
f.	Do_____	*Twelve*
g.	U______	*One*
h.	Se_____	*Seven*
i.	No_____	*Nine*
j.	Di_____	*Ten*

3. Complete the sentences with the missing words below

a.	Ho ___________ anni.	*I am seven years old.*
b.	Mi ___________ Dylan.	*My name is Dylan.*
c.	Ho ___________ anni.	*I am eleven years old.*
d.	Come _____ chiami?	*What is your name?*
e.	Quanti anni _____ ?	*What age are you?*
f.	_________, mi chiamo Patrizia.	*Hello, my name is Patricia.*
g.	Come ti ________ ?	*What is your name?*
h.	Mi chiamo Anna e _____ sei anni.	*My name is Anna and I am 6.*

hai	chiami	ho	ti	Ciao	undici	sette	chiamo

4. Sentence Building Blocks

Use the words in the building blocks to make a correct Italian sentence

a. cinque | anni | Ho ___________________

b. hai? | anni | Quanti ___________________

c. dodici | e | Mi | ho | Gianni | anni | chiamo ___________________

d. Carlo | e | undici | ho | chiamo | anni | Mi ___________________

Unit 1. My name and age: READING

1. Sylla-Bees

   Translate the phrases putting the cells in the correct order

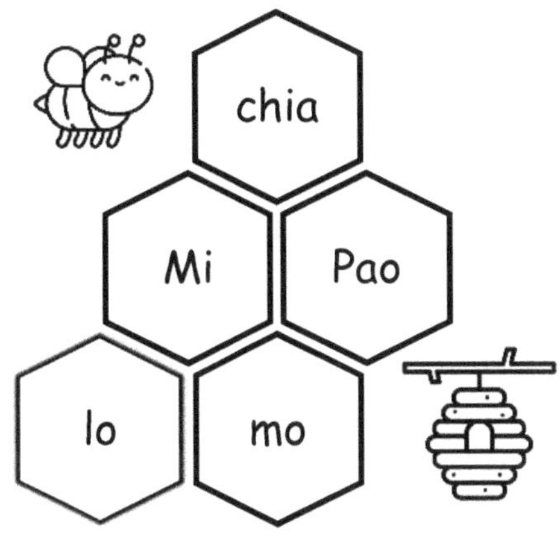

a. *My name is Paolo.*

M __ c __ __ __ __ __ P__ __ __ __

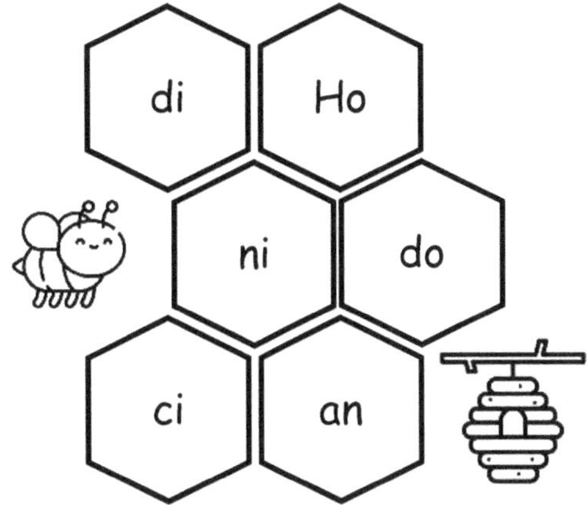

b. *I am 12 years old.*

Ho   d __ __ __ __ __ a __ __ __

c. *I am 11 years old.*

__ __ __ __ __ __ __ __

__ __ __ __ __

THE LANGUAGE GYM

	True	False
1a. His name is **Roberto**.		
1b. Her name is **Carla**.		
1c. He is 11 years old.		
1d. She is 8 years old.		
2a. His name is **PierPaolo**.		
2b. Her name is **Amira**.		
2c. He is 12 years old.		
2d. She is 10 years old.		

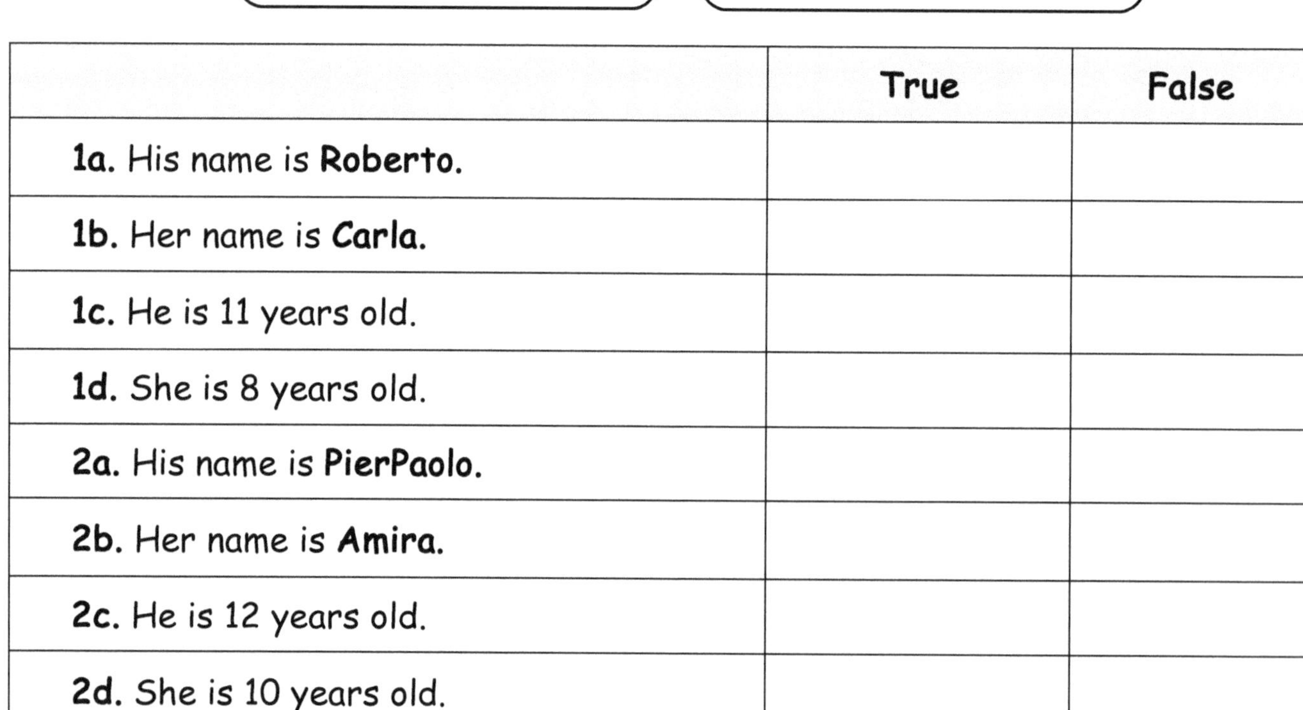

Unit 1. My name and age: WRITING

1. Spelling

a. M __ c __ __ __ __ __ Luca   *My name is Luca.*

b. Ci __ __, h __ d __ eci an __ __   *Hello, I am ten years old.*

c. H __ q __ __ ttro __ __ ni   *I am four years old.*

d. H __ n __ __ e a __ __ __   *I am nine years old.*

e. Co __ __ t __ ch __ __ __ i?   *What's your name?*

f. Qua __ __ __ a __ __ __ ha __?   *How old are you?*

g. B __ __ __ gior __ __, h __ t __ __ anni *Good morning, I am three.*

2. Anagrams: unscramble the Italian

a. iaCo oh ret anin   *Hello, I am 3 years old.*

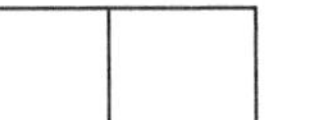 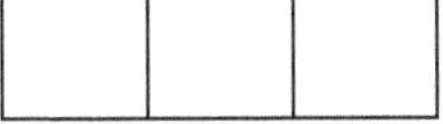 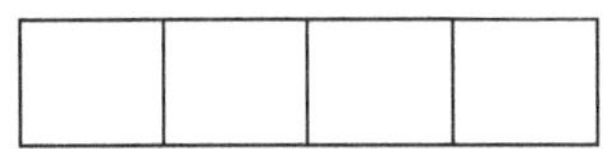

b. iM achiom aMiar   *My name is Maria.*

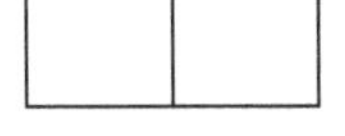

c. oH odidic inan   *I am twelve years old.*

  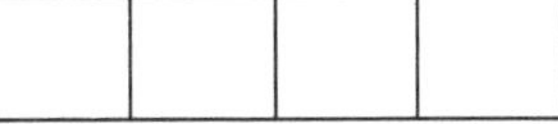

d. Ho diciun inna   *I am eleven years old.*

 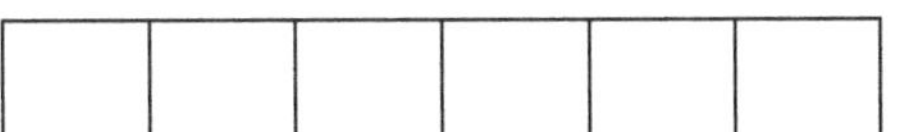 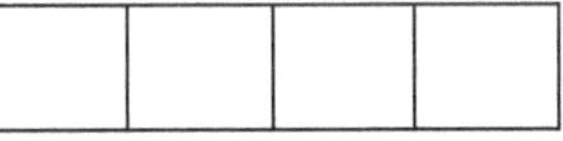

e. iCao ho ise iann   *Ciao, I am six years old.*

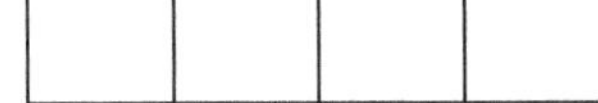   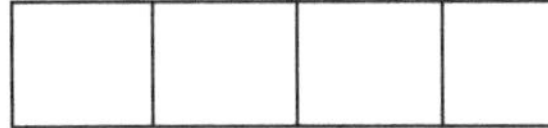

3. Faulty Translation. Write the correct English version.

e.g. Ho _dieci_ anni. ⟹ I am _11_ years old. | I am 10 years old |

a. Ho sette anni. ⟹ I am 6 years old. | |

b. Quanti anni hai? ⟹ What's your name? | |

c. Come ti chiami? ⟹ How old are you? | |

d. Buongiorno Laura. ⟹ Good evening Laura. | |

e. Buonasera Fabio. ⟹ Good morning Fabio. | |

4. Phrase-level Translation. How would you say it in Italian?

a. I am 8 years old. _______________________________

b. My name is Mario _______________________________

c. What's your name? _______________________________

d. I am 12 years old. _______________________________

e. How old are you? _______________________________

f. Good morning. _______________________________

g. Hello. _______________________________

h. Good evening. _______________________________

UNIT 2
L'ALFABETO

In this unit you will learn to:

- ✓ Spell your name in Italian
- ✓ Practise Italian sounds

You will revisit:

- ★ Saying your name and age
- ★ How to count from 1 to 12

THE LANGUAGE GYM

UNIT 2. ALPHABET AND PHONICS.
I can hear and pronounce Italian sounds

Come si scrive il tuo nome? *How do you spell your name?*

1. Listen and write the alphabet as you hear it.

Il mio nome si scrive

My name is spelt

A	<ah>	N	__________
B	__________	O	__________
C	__________	P	__________
D	__________	Q	__________
E	__________	R	__________
F	__________	S	__________
G	__________	T	__________
H	__________	U	__________
I	__________	V	__________
J	__________	W	__________
K	__________	X	__________
L	__________	Y	__________
M	__________	Z	__________

***Author's notes:** In the actual Italian alphabet there are no j,k,w,x,y. They only exist as non official letters, we have included them for reference.

2. Fill in the gaps: Come si scrive? *How is it spelt?*

a. C __ r l o

b. F i l __ p p o

c. __ i u l i a

d. A l e __ s a n d r o

e. C r __ s t i n a

f. L e t i __ i a

g. S o __ i a

h. P __ e t r o

i. G i o __ a n n i

j. V a __ e r i a

3. Complete the words with the missing letters

a. Com__ s__ scriv__ i__ t__o n__me?

b. Mi chi__mo __aria.

c. M__ chiamo V__leria.

d. I__ m__ nom__ si s__rive.

e. Mi ch__amo __iovanni.

4. Listen and choose the correct spelling

	1	2
a.	Mi chiamo	Mi ghiamo
b.	anni	ani
c.	Sofia	Sophia
d.	compleanno	cumplianno
e.	Italiano	Italieno
f.	Julia	Giulia
g.	Giovanni	Jovanni
h.	giallo	gialo
i.	bambino	bampino
j.	gnomo	niomo

THE LANGUAGE GYM

5. Listen and tick what you hear

1.	B	P	T
2.	S	Z	H
3.	L	H	J
4.	L	N	M
5.	I	E	A
6.	T	D	P
7.	X	H	V
8.	U	V	B
9.	U	O	I

6. Listen and write the names being spelled out:

1. _ _ _ _ _ _

2. _ _ _ _ _ _

3. _ _ _ _

4. _ _ _ _ _

5. _ _ _ _ _

6. _ _ _ _ _ _ _

7. _ _ _ _ _ _ _ _ _

8. _ _ _ _ _ _ _

THE LANGUAGE GYM

No Snakes No Ladders

PARTENZA	1 Ciao	2 Mi chiamo Martina	3 Mi chiamo Carlo	4 Come ti chiami?	5 Buongiorno	6 Mi chiamo Pietro	7 e
15 Mi chiamo Patrizia	14 Ho otto anni	13 Quanti anni hai?	12 Ho nove anni	11 Ho undici anni	10 Mi chiamo Maria	9 Mi chiamo Filippo	8 Ho sette anni
16 Ho dieci anni	17 Mi chiamo Luca	18 Come si scrive?	19 Buona-sera	20 Ho cinque anni	21 Mi chiamo Sofia	22 Ho sei anni	23 Ciao mi chiamo Anna
ARRIVO	30 Buon giorno Maria	29 Ciao Simone	28 Ho quattro anni	27 Mi chiamo Carlo	26 Ciao, mi chiamo Nicola	25 Buongiorno, ho dodici anni	24 Mi chiamo Giulio

No Snakes No Ladders

PARTENZA	1 Hello	2 My name is Martina	3 My name is Carlo	4 What's your name?	5 Good morning	6 My name is Pietro	7 and
15 My name is Patrizia	14 I am 8 years old	13 How old are you?	12 I am 9 years old	11 I am 11 years old	10 My name is Maria	9 My name is Filippo	8 I am 7 years old
16 I am 10 years old	17 My name is Luca	18 How do you spell it?	19 Good afternoon	20 I am 5 years old	21 My name is Sofia	22 I am 6 years old	23 Hello, my name is Anna
ARRIVO	30 Good morning Maria	29 Hello Simone	28 I am 4 years old	27 My name is Carlo	26 My name is Nicola	25 Good morning, I am 12 years old	24 My name is Giulio

UNIT 3
COME STAI?

In this unit you will learn how to say in Italian:

✓ How you are

You will revisit:

★ What is your name
★ Saying your age
★ 'Hello' and 'Good morning'

THE LANGUAGE GYM

UNIT 3. COME STAI?
I can greet and say how I am

Come stai? *How are you?*

				MASCULINE 	FEMININE
Ciao *Hello*		**benissimo** *great*			
Buongiorno *Good morning*		**molto bene** *very well*		**annoiato** *bored*	**annoiata** *bored*
Buon pomeriggio *Good afternoon*	**sto** *I feel*	**bene** *well*		**contento** *cheerful*	**contenta** *cheerful*
			perché sono *because I am*	**felice** *happy*	**felice** *happy*
		così così *so-so*			
Buonasera *Good evening*	**non sto** *I don't feel*	**male** *bad*		**nervoso** *nervous*	**nervosa** *nervous*
Buonanotte *Good night*				**stanco** *tired*	**stanca** *tired*
		molto male *very bad*		**stressato** *stressed*	**stressata** *stressed*
Grazie *Thank you* **E tu?** *And you?*		**malissimo** *awful*		**tranquillo** *calm* **triste** *sad*	**tranquilla** *calm* **triste** *sad*

Author's note: **"sto"** *means* **"I feel"**. *It is often used to talk about how you are feeling or how you are.*

THE LANGUAGE GYM

Unit 3. I can greet and say how I am: LISTENING 

1. Listen and tick the word you hear 

	1	2	3
e.g.	*Buongiorno*	*Grazie*	*Buonasera*
a.	Malisimo	Malissimo	Male
b.	Tranquilo	Tranquillo	Tranquilla
c.	Contento	Continto	Contenta
d.	Stanco	Stanca	Stanko
e.	Stressata	Stresata	Stressato

2. Listen and complete with the missing vowels

a. S__no content__.

b. Buon__notte.

c. Son__ tranquill__.

d. Sono tr__nquill__.

e. Sto b__nissimo.

f. Son__ trist__.

g. S__no stanc__.

h. Ciao, m__ chi__mo Roberto.

i. Sto molto ben__.

j. Buonaser__.

k. St__ maliss__mo.

l. Sono ann__iato.

m. Sono annoiat__.

n. Buong__orno.

a
e
i
o
u

3. Complete with the missing syllables in the box below

a. _ _ _ molto bene.

b. Sto be _ _ ssimo.

c. Buon _ _ _ _ no.

d. Buona _ _ ra, sto ma _ _.

e. _ _ no contento

f. Sono feli _ _ .

g. Sto bene per _ _ _ sono tranquil _ _.

h. Sono anno_ _ta.

i. Sto malis _ _ mo.

j. _ _ _ _ o, sto be _ _ _ .

k. Buo _ _ sera, sto ma _ _ ssimo.

l. Sto così co _ _ , buona _ _ tte.

ce Cia ia se si sì So le li lo
na ne ni no gior Sto chè

4. Listen and choose the correct spelling

	1	2
a.	Sono felice	Sono feliche
b.	Buonjorno	Buongiorno
c.	Buonanotte	Buonanote
d.	Nervouso	Nervoso
e.	Sto benissimo	Sto benisimo
f.	Sono tranquilo	Sono tranquillo
g.	Sto male	Sto mali
h.	Sono annoiata	Sono anoiata
i.	Comi stai?	Come stai?
j.	Sto bene, grazie	Sto bene, grazi

5. Break the flow: Draw a line between words

a. Buongiorno, stomoltobene. Etu?

b. Buonasera, michiamoRobertoestobene

c. Ciao, stomalissimoperchèsonostanco

d. MichiamoCarloestomaleperchèsonotriste

e. Stobenissimoperchèsonocontento

f. Sonounpo'annoiato. Etu, comestai?

g. Ciao, stomoltobeneperchèsonocontento

h. Sonomoltostancobuonanotte

6. Fill in the grid with the correct information in English

	Greeting	Emotion
e.g. Paola	*Hello*	*Happy*
a. Nicola		
b. Daniele		
c. Francesca		
d. Marco		
e. Bea		

7. Faulty Echo

e.g. Ciao, sto molto bene.

a. Buongiorno, sono contento.

b. Sto bene perché sono felice.

c. Sto molto male perché sono annoiata.

d. Come stai? Sto benissimo.

e. Sto male perché sono triste.

f. Sto bene perché sono calmo.

g. Buongiorno, sono triste.

h. Buonasera, mi chiamo Simone.

i. Ciao, sto malissimo. E tu?

8. Spot the Intruder

Identify the word in each sentence the speaker is NOT saying

e.g. Sto molto bene, grazie.

a. Buonasera, sto sono molto bene.

b. Buongiorno, sto molto così così.

c. Mi sto bene perché sono felice.

d. Ciao, sto benissimo perché sono contento contenta.

e. Come sto stai? Sto male.

f. Come ti stai? Sto benissimo.

g. Sto male perché sono sto triste.

9. Narrow Listening - Gap-fill

a. Ciao, sto _____________ perché sono felice.

b. Buongiorno, sto benissimo perché sono _____________.

c. Buonasera, _________ male perché sono _____________.

d. Come _________? Sto molto bene, _____________.

e. Ciao, _________ benissimo perché sono _____________.

f. Come stai? Sto _____________ perché sono felice.

g. Ciao mi _________ Francesca e sono contenta e _____________.

Unit 3. I can greet and say how I am: VOCAB BUILDING 

1. Match Up

1. Stanco
2. Annoiata
3. Sto
4. Sono
5. Nervosa
6. Tranquillo
7. Felice
8. Contento
9. Come stai?

a. Bored
b. How are you?
c. Calm
d. Happy
e. Tired
f. I am
g. Cheerful
h. Nervous
i. I feel

1	
2	
3	
4	
5	
6	
7	
8	
9	

2. Broken Words

a. Così __________   *So-so*

b. Benis__________   *Great*

c. Malis__________   *Awful*

d. Sto be_______   *I feel well*

e. Buon_______no   *Good morning*

f. Ci__________   *Hello*

g. Per__________   *Because*

h. Sono ___tento   *I am happy*

i. M_______ bene   *Very well*

3. Complete with the missing words

a. Sto _____________ perché sono felice. *I feel great because I am happy.*

b. _______ male perché sono stanca.   *I feel bad because I am tired.*

c. Sto bene ___________ sono contenta. *I feel well because I am cheerful.*

d. Sto così così perché sono ___________. *I feel so-so because I am sad.*

e. Mi chiamo Teresa ____ sto bene.   *My name is Teresa and I feel well.*

f. Come _______? Sto molto male perché sono _______________.

How are you? I feel very well because I am bored.

stai	e	Sto	benissimo	triste	perchè	annoiato

Unit 3. I can greet and say how I am: READING

1. Sylla-bees
Translate the phrases putting the cells in the correct order

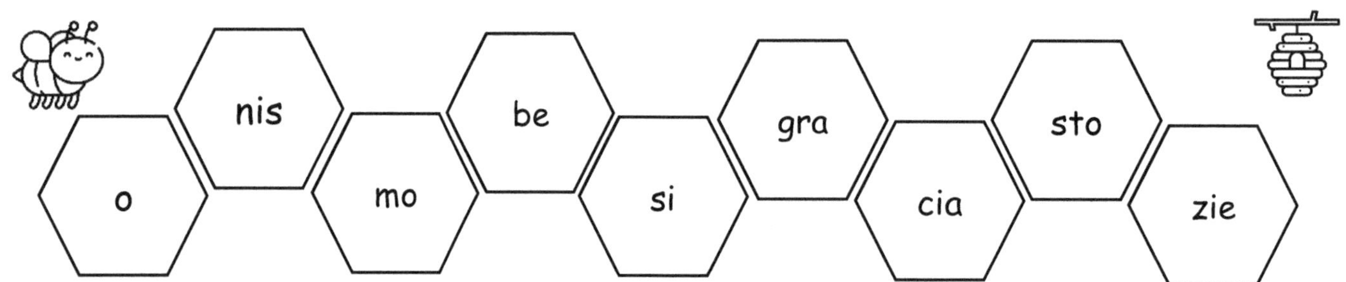

a. *Hello, I feel great, thank you.*
C_________, s______ b______________, g___________.

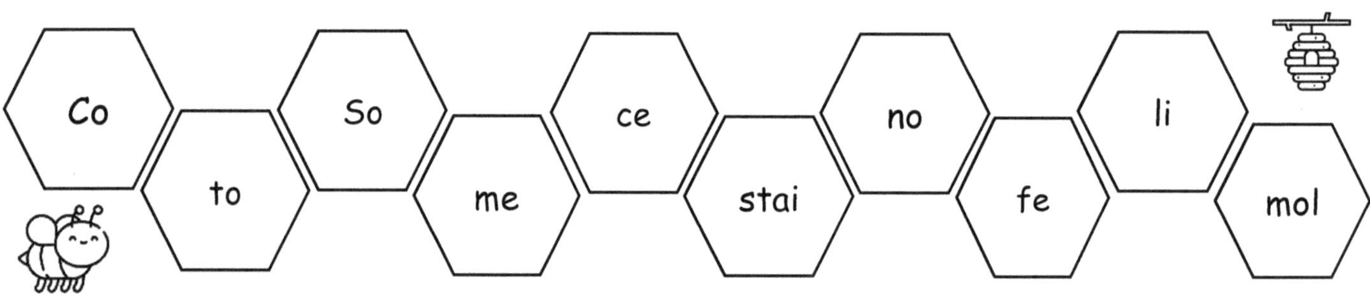

b. *How are you? I feel very happy.*
C_________ s_______? S________ m_________ f__________.

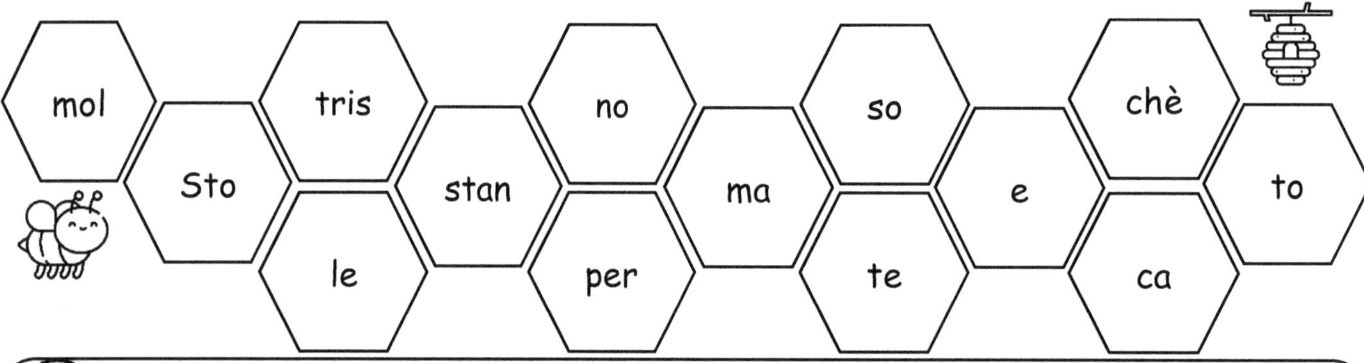

c. *I feel very bad because I am sad and tired (f).*
S______ m__________ m_________ p___________ s__________
t__________ e s__________.

THE LANGUAGE GYM

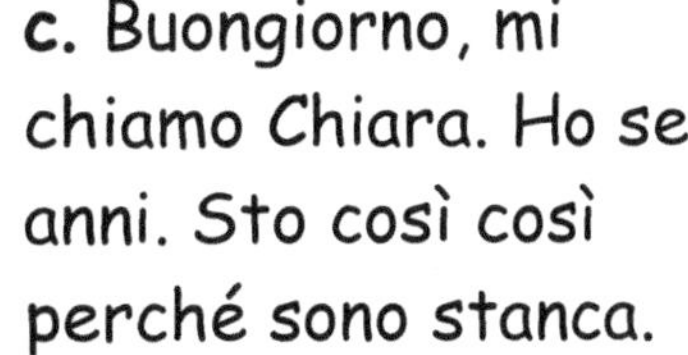

e.g. Ciao, mi chiamo Enrico. Ho cinque anni. Sto molto bene perché sono felice.

c. Buongiorno, mi chiamo Chiara. Ho sei anni. Sto così così perché sono stanca.

a. Ciao, mi chiamo Amira. Ho undici anni. Sto benissimo perché sono contenta.

d. Ciao, mi chiamo Simona. Ho nove anni. Sto bene perché sono tranquilla.

b. Buongiorno, mi chiamo Matteo. Ho tredici anni. Sto male perché sono annoiato.

e. Ciao, mi chiamo Roberto. Ho dodici anni. Sto male perché sono nervoso.

	Name	Age	Feeling	Reason
e.g.	Enrico	5	Very well	Happy
a.				
b.				
c.				
d.				
e.				

Unit 3. I can greet and say how I am: WRITING

1. Spelling

a. S __ __   m __ __   t __   be __ __.   *I feel very well.*

b. S __ __   b __ n __ ss __ m __.   *I feel great.*

c. P__ __ ch __   s __ __ __ __   fel __ __ __.   *Because I am happy.*

d. Pe __ __ __ è s __ n __ tr __ __ __ __ __.   *Because I am sad.*

e. __ e __ __ h __ __ on __ an __ oi __ __ a.   *Because I am bored.*

f. C __ __ e __ t __ __?   *How are you?*

g. C __ m __ s __ __ i? Sto m __ __ __.   *How are you? I feel bad.*

2. Anagrams: unscramble the Italian

a. tSo   nimossibe.   *I feel great.*

b. iM achiom   oemnSi.   *My name is Simone.*

c. nooS tonoaina.   *I am bored.*

d. onN soon eclife.   *I am not happy.*

e. toS oltom   eenb.   *I feel very well.*

3. Faulty Translation. Spot the difference and correct with English words.

e.g. Sono <u>stanca</u>. ⟹ I am <u>cheerful</u>.　　| *I am tired* |

a. Sto molto bene.　⟹ I am happy.

b. Come stai?　⟹ What's your name?

c. Sono annoiata.　⟹ I am nervous.

d. Sono triste.　⟹ I am bored.

e. Buongiorno, come stai? ⟹ Hello, how are you?

4. Phrase-level Translation.
How would you say it in Italian?

a. I am well. _______________________________________

b. I am awful._______________________________________

c. How are you? _____________________________________

d. I am bored. (m) __________________________________

e. I am stressed. (m) _______________________________

f. I am cheerful. (f)_______________________________

g. Hello, I am great. _______________________________

h. I am calm. (f) ___________________________________

i. I am cheerful. (f)_______________________________

UNIT 4

IL MIO COMPLEANNO

In this unit you will learn how to say in Italian:

- ✓ When your birthday is
- ✓ Numbers up to 31
- ✓ Months of the year

You will revisit:

- ★ Your name and age
- ★ Saying how you are

UNIT 4. IL MIO COMPLEANNO
I can say when my birthday is

Quando è il tuo compleanno? *When is your birthday?*

		un	1*	anno *year*
		due	2	
		tre	3	
		quattro	4	
		cinque	5	
		sei	6	
Mi chiamo	ho	sette	7	anni *years*
I am called	*I have*	otto	8	
		nove	9	
		dieci	10	
		undici	11	
		dodici	12	
		tredici	13	
		quattordici	14	
		quindici	15	

	sedici	16		
	diciasette	17		
	diciotto	18	gennaio	*January*
	diciannove	19	febbraio	*February*
	venti	20	marzo	*March*
Il mio compleanno è il	ventuno	21	aprile	*April*
My birthday is on the	ventidue	22	maggio	*May*
	ventitrè	23	giugno	*June*
	ventiquattro	24	luglio	*July*
	venticinque	25	agosto	*August*
	ventisei	26	settembre	*September*
	ventisette	27	ottobre	*October*
	ventotto	28	novembre	*November*
	ventinove	29	dicembre	*December*
	trenta	30		
	trentuno	31		

***Author's note:**

When "**il**" preceeds a vowel it changes into "**l'**" **e.g.** l'uno/l'otto/l'undici marzo.

To say your birthday is on the 1st you can say "il primo" or "l'uno".

E.g. **Il mio compleanno è il primo / l'uno agosto** *My birthday is on 1ˢᵗ August*

Unit 4. I can say when my birthday is: LISTENING

1. Listen and tick the word you hear 

	1	2	3
a.	Sei	Sette	Tre
b.	Giugno	Luglio	Uno
c.	Sedici	Diciasette	Diciotto
d.	Ventidue	Ventiquattro	Ventinove
e.	Settembre	Novembre	Dicembre
f.	Anni	Compleanno	Anno

2. Faulty Echo

***e.g.** Ho <u>dieci</u> anni.*

a. Il mio compleanno è...

b. Il diciannove febbraio.

c. Mi chiamo Mario.

d. Il ventisei marzo.

e. Il diciotto ottobre.

f. Ho nove anni.

g. Il quattro dicembre.

h. Il tredici agosto.

3. Listen and complete with the missing letters

a. Il dodi__i mar__o.

b. Il __uattordici feb__raio.

c. Il tredi__i lu__lio.

d. Il vent__sei l__glio.

e. Il vent__ april__.

f. Il q__indic__ o__tobre.

g. __o cinq__e an__i.

h. Il trent__ __ennaio.

4. Complete with the missing syllables in the box below

a. Ho _ _ _ ci anni.

b. Il ven _ _ _ to set _ _ _ bre.

c. Il tren _ _ no _ _ glio.

d. Il mio _ _ _ pleanno è...

e. Il di _ _ _ _ sette agosto.

f. Il dodi _ _ giu _ _ _.

g. Il _ _ _ _ tro mar _ _.

h. Il tre _ _ _ naio.

i. Il venticin _ _ _ mag _ _ _.

j. Il _ _ _ _ ta apri _ _.

zo	gno	die	com	tem	cias	gio	ci
gen	lu	tu	tot	quat	que	tren	le

5. Break the flow: Draw a line between words

a. Ilmiocompleannoèildiciassettenovembre.

b. MichiamoMariaehoundicianni.

c. Quand'èiltuocompleanno?

d. Ilmiocompleannoèilventiduedicembre.

e. Cometichiami?MichiamoRitaehosetteanni.

f. Ilmiocompleannoèiltredicifebbraio.

g. Hoseiannieilmiocompleannoèilduemaggio.

h. Ciaoilmiocompleannoèilprimosettembre.

i. MichiamoDanieleestomoltobenegrazie.

6. Fill in the grid with the correct date of birth 

	Day	Month
e.g.	*12th*	*April*
a.		
b.		
c.		
d.		
e.		
f.		

7. Spot the Intruder 

Identify the word in each sentence the speaker is NOT saying

e.g. Il mio compleanno è il <u>tre</u> sette giugno.

a. Il mio compleanno è e il diciannove dicembre.

b. Il mio compleanno è il venti ventuno gennaio.

c. Quand' è ho il tuo compleanno?

d. Il mio tuo nome è Paola. Il mio compleanno è il due febbraio.

e. Il mio compleanno è il quindici cinque giugno.

f. Il mio compleanno è il trentuno trenta ottobre.

g. Mi chiamo Antonella. Il mio compleanno è il quattro quattordici aprile.

h. Il mio compleanno è il cinque luglio giugno.

8. Catch it, Swap it: rewrite the wrong word

e.g. *Il ventisette <u>dicembre</u>.* | *novembre*

a. Ho dodici anni.

b. Il mio compleanno è il venti luglio.

c. Il trentuno ottobre.

d. Ho dieci anni.

e. Il tredici aprile.

f. Il quattro agosto.

g. Il sei luglio.

h. Sto molto bene.

9. Listen, Tick or Cross

	✓	✗
e.g. *Davide's birthday is the 9th December.*	✓	
a. Francesco is 13 years old.		
b. Marta's birthday is the 7th June.		
c. Giulia is 15 years old. Her birthday is the 8th May.		
d. Antonio's birthday is on the 17th November.		
e. Dylan's birthday is the 18th October.		
f. Gianfranco's birthday is on the 15th July.		

Unit 4. I can say when my birthday is: READING

1. Sylla-Bees
   Translate the phrases putting the cells in the correct order

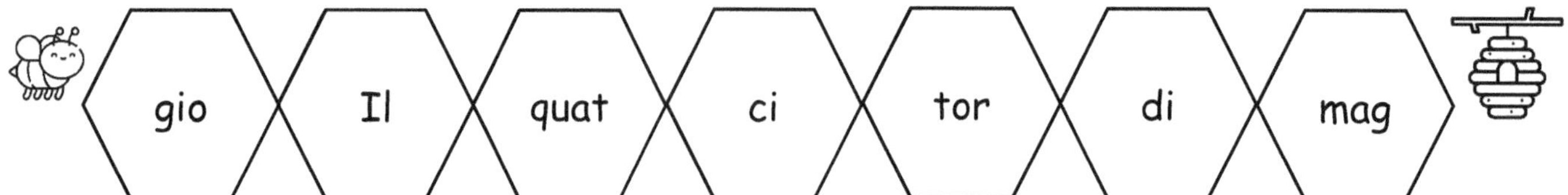

a. *The 14th of May.*
I__ q_________ m_________ .

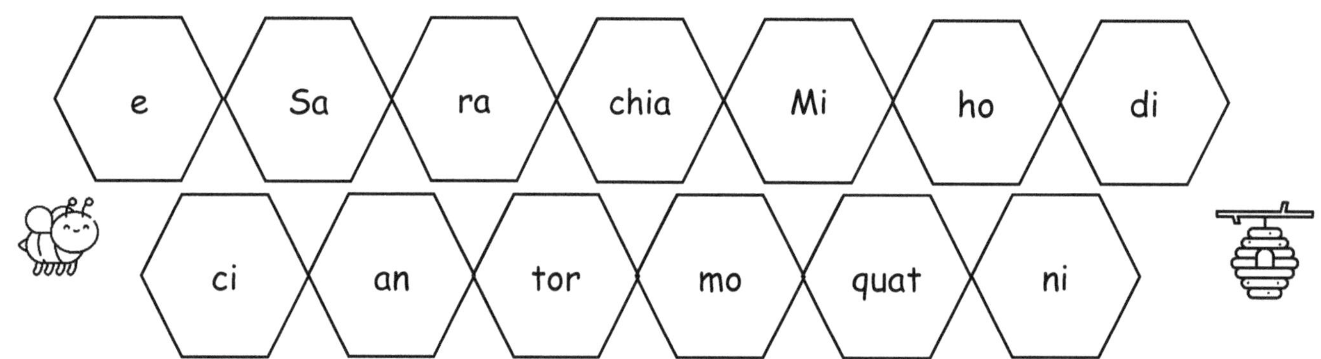

b. *My name is Sara and I am 14 years old.*
M__ c_________ S______ e h__ q_________ a______ .

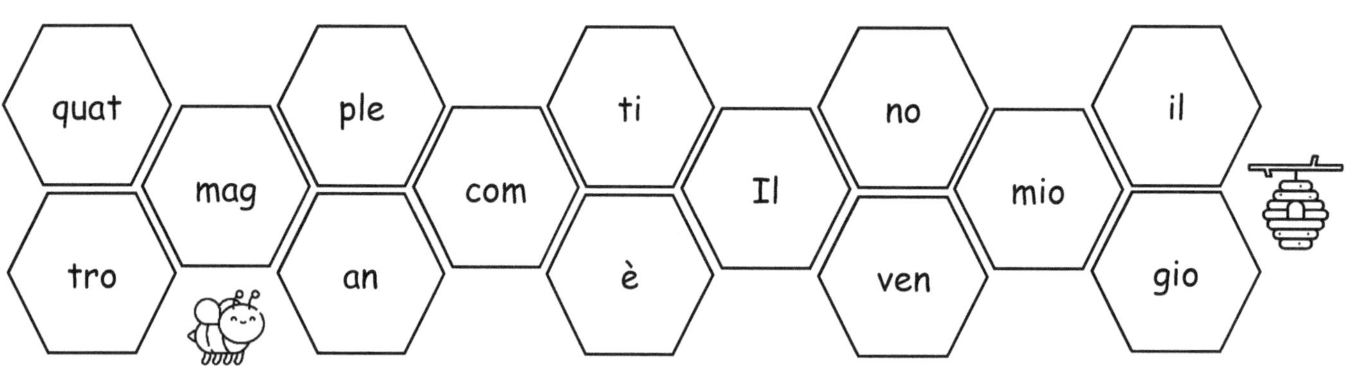

c. *My birthday is on the 24th of May.*
I__ m___ c____________ è i__ v___________ m________ .

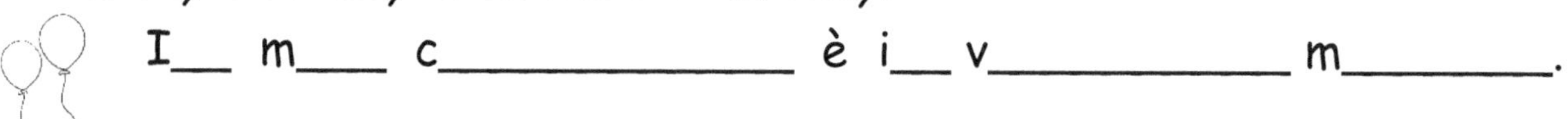

THE LANGUAGE GYM

2. True or False
Read the paragraphs below and then answer True or False

		True	False
1	a. Her name is **Sara.**		
	b. She says hi		
	c. She is great because she is happy.		
	d. She is 6 years old.		
	e. Her birthday is on the 13th of October.		
2	a. His name is **Leonardo.**		
	b. He says good morning		
	c. He is awful because he is nervous.		
	d. He is 10 years old.		
	e. His birthday is on the 3rd of February.		

3. Tick or Cross

A. Put a tick if you find the words in the text or a cross if you do not find them.

Ciao, mi chiamo **Beatrice**. Sto bene perché sono tranquilla. Ho sette anni. Il mio compleanno è il ventuno settembre.

Ciao mi chiamo **Daniela**. Sto molto male perché sono triste. Ho nove anni. Il mio compleanno è il ventiquattro luglio.

	✓	✗
a. Mi chiamo		
b. Dodici anni		
c. Ciao		
d. Sto male		
e. Il mio compleanno		
f. Il venti settembre		

g. I am 7 years old		
h. My birthday		
i. 24th July		
j. Because I am happy		
k. I am stressed		

B. Find the Italian in the texts above

a. My name is ____

b. My birthday is ____

c. I am 7 years old ____

d. ...because I am calm (f)____

4. Language Detective

- <u>Mi chiamo</u> **Angelo** Benedetti. Sto bene perché sono felice. Ho dodici anni. Il mio compleanno è il quattro giugno.

- Buon pomeriggio. Mi chiamo **Pamela** Colangeli. Sto male perché sono stressata. Ho tredici anni. Il mio compleanno è il quattro luglio.

- Ciao, sono **Giulio** Leggeri. Sto bene perché sono contento. Ho quattordici anni. Il mio compleanno è l'undici luglio.

- Buongiorno. Mi chiamo **Alessandro** Cimato. Sto così così perché sono stanco. Ho dieci anni. Il mio compleanno è il trenta ottobre.

A. Find someone who…

a. …is 12 years old.

b. …is tired.

c. …is happy.

d. …was born on the 30th October.

e. …is 13 years old.

f. …is cheerful.

g. …was born on the 4th July.

h. …is 14 years old.

i. …was born the 11th of July.

j. …was born the 4th of June.

B. Put a cross in the box and underline the corresponding Italian translation. One is odd.

My name is (crossed out)	I am 14 years old	I am bad
Good morning	My birthday	Hello, I am
because I am stressed	I am cheerful	30th October
I am great	Good afternoon	I am 11 years old
11th July	I am so-so	I am happy

1. Spelling

a. B__ __ng__ __r__o .   *Good morning.*

b. I__   m__o __ __ __ __lea__ __ __.*My birthday.*

c. Il t__e__i__i no__em__ __e.   *The 13th of November.*

d. __l __ __n__ __ __ ap__ __l__.   *The 5th of April.*

e. Il tre__ __ __i __en__ __ __o.   *The 13th of January.*

f. Il q__ __ndi__ __ __ __g__io.   *The 15th of July.*

g. __o q__ __ttor__ __ __i a__n__.   *I am 14 years old.*

2. Anagrams: unscramble the Italian

a. lI etste totorbe   *7th of October.*

b. Il ciditre gostao   *13th of August.*

c. L' diciun cembredi   *11th of December.*

d. Il tantre gnogiu   *30th of June.*

3. Gapped Translation

Complete the translation

a. Ho sette anni   .   *I am ___________ years old.*

b. Buongiorno, Ho sei anni.   *_______________, I am ______ years old.*

c. Ciao, Non sono stanco.   *Hi, I am not _____________.*

d. Ciao, sto molto bene.   *Hi, I am _______ _________.*

e. Il sedici febbraio.   *The ___________ of February.*

f. Il veintitrè agosto.   *The ___________ of August.*

g. Ho otto anni.   *I am ______ years old.*

4. Split Sentences

a. Mi chiamo	**1.** il dodici aprile.
b. Sto	**2.** undici anni.
c. Ho	**3.** Paolo Bianchi.
d. Il mio compleanno è	**4.** sono stanca.
e. Sto così così perchè	**5.** tuo compleanno?
f. Quando è il	**6.** benissimo.
g. Come	**7.** ti chiami?

a	b	c	d	e	f	g
3						

5. Rock Climbing

Starting from the bottom, pick one chunk from each row to translate the sentences below.

	a.	b.	c.	d.	e.
	gennaio.	il ventitrè giugno.	Ho dieci anni.	luglio.	il tre maggio.
	compleanno è	è il cinque	Il mio compleanno è	marzo.	È il cinque
	il ventotto	Francesco.	il tuo compleanno?	anni. Il mio	Il mio compleanno
	Mi chiamo	Ho dodici	Il mio compleanno è	Ho undici anni.	Quando è
	a.	b.	c.	d.	e.

a. My name is Francesco. My birthday is on the 3rd May.

____

b. I am 12 years old. My birthday is on the 23rd of June.

____

c. My birthday is on the 28th March. I am 10 years old.

____

d. I am 11 years old. My birthday is on the 5th of July.

____

e. When is your birthday? It's on the 15th of January.

____

6. Mosaic Translation

Use the words in the grid to help you translate the sentences below.

a.	Ho tredici anni.	Il mio compleanno	Ho	ventidue	dicembre.
b.	Quanti	Il mio	è il	il sedici	undici anni.
c.	Mi chiamo Anna.	è il trentuno	È	ho	aprile.
d.	Quando è	anni hai?	compleanno è il	dodici	agosto.
e.	Il mio compleanno	il tuo compleanno?	ottobre e	diciotto	anni.

a. I am 13 years old. My birthday is on the 18th of April.

____

b. How old are you? I am 12 years old.

____

c. My name is Anna. My birthday is on the 22th of August.

____

d. When is your birthday? It's on the 16th of December.

____

e. My birthday is on the 31st of October and I am 11 years old.

____

7. Sentence Puzzle

Put the words in the correct order

a. è compleanno Il mio settembre il tredici

b. tuo Quando compleanno è tuo il?

c. aprile Il compleanno mio il dodici è

d. chiamo Mi Carlo nove e ho anni

e. mio Il gennaio compleanno il diciannove è

f. il dicembre mio Il è compleanno ventiquattro

g. chiamo Mi Chiara ho anni quattordici e

h. chiamo Maria il è dodici il gennaio mio compleanno e Mi

i. Quanti Ho anni anni sette hai?

8. Tangled Translation

a. Write the Italian words in English to complete the translation

Hello, **mi chiamo** Filippo. **Sto** very well **perché sono** happy. **Ho** ten **anni.**

Il mio compleanno is **il venti** of January. When is **il tuo compleanno?**

b. Write the English words in Italian to complete the translation

Ciao, **my name is** Gisella. **I am** male **because** sono **tired. I am** undici **years old.**

My birthday è l'otto **July.** Quando è **your birthday?**

9. Fill in the Gaps

a. Ciao, mi __________ Alessandro. Sto __________ perché __________ contento. Ho quattordici __________. Il mio compleanno è il __________ ottobre.

bene	quindici	anni	chiamo	sono

b. Ciao, mi chiamo Romina. __________ nove anni. Sto male __________ sono __________. Il mio compleanno _____ il ventidue __________.

triste	è	ho	febbraio	perché

10. Guided Translation

a. M__ c______ S________ e h___ u______ a______.

My name is Simona and I am 11 years old.

b. S_____ m_____ b_____ p_______ s_______ c__________.

I am very well because I am cheerful. (m)

c. N___ s______ b____ p_______ s______ s__________.

I am not well because I am tired. (f)

d. I__ m____ c___________ è i___ q________ a________.

My birthday is on the 15th of August.

e. Q________ è i___ t___ c_______________?

When is your birthday?

11. Pyramid Translation

Translate into Italian starting from the top. Write the sentences in the grid below.

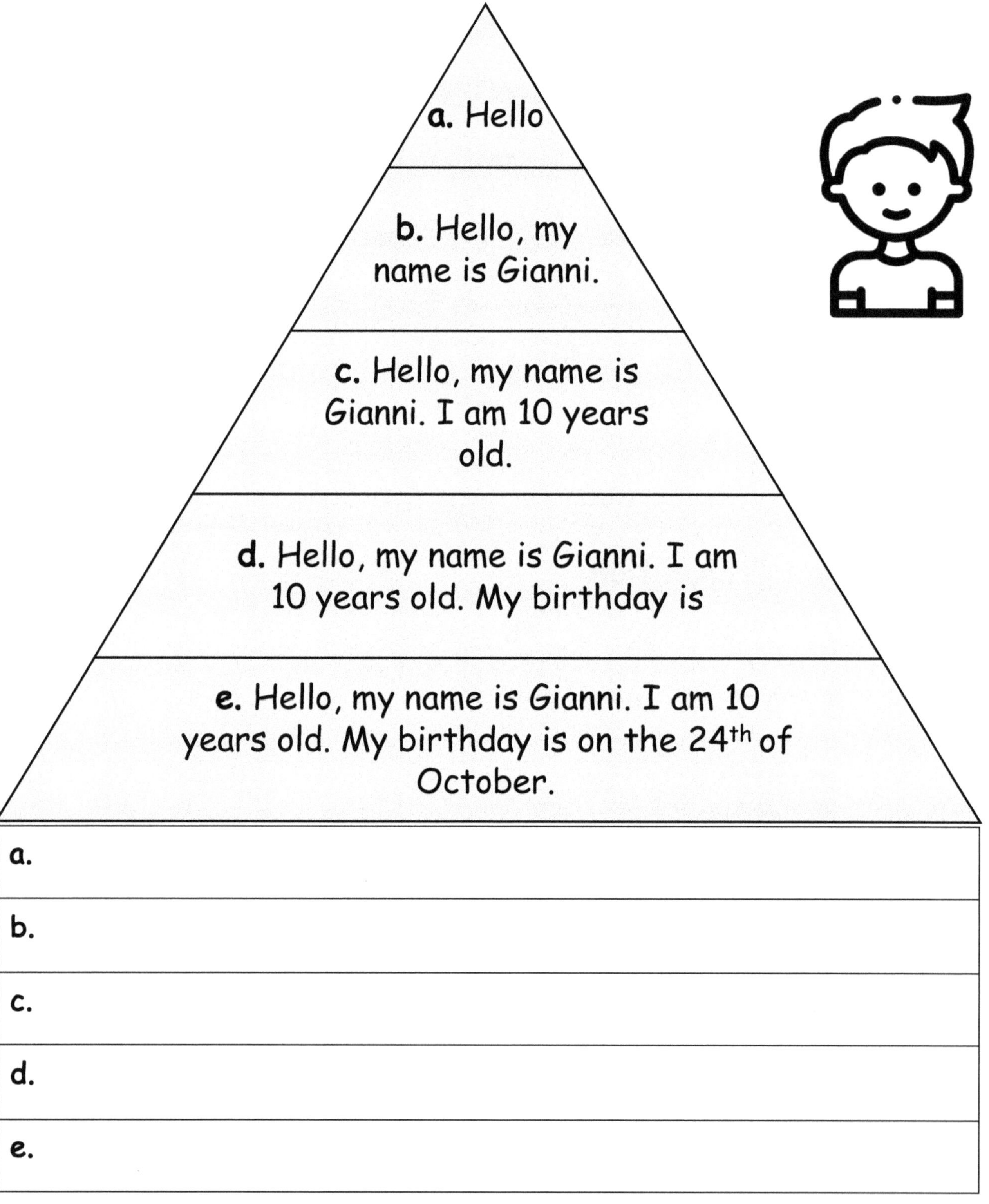

a.	
b.	
c.	
d.	
e.	

 # No Snakes No Ladders

 PARTENZA	1 Mi chiamo Gianni	2 Ho dodci anni	3 Ciao. Come stai?	4 Sto molto bene	5 Sto così così	6 Perché sono stanco	7 Come ti chiami?
15 Il mio compleanno è	14 Però sono nervosa	13 Perchè sono annoiata	12 Sto benissimo	11 Ho dodici anni	10 Quanti anni hai?	9 Sono felice	8 Sono stressato
16 Il venti maggio	17 l'undici giugno	18 Quando è il tuo compleanno?	19 Non sono triste	20 Sto male	21 Il trentuno ottobre	22 Ho nove anni	23 Grazie
 ARRIVO	30 Buonasera, sto malissimo	29 Sono contento	28 Ho quindici anni	27 Il trenta gennaio	26 Perchè sono tranquilla	25 Buongiorno, sto così così	24 Il ventisei luglio

THE LANGUAGE GYM

No Snakes No Ladders

PARTENZA	1 My name is Gianni	2 I am 12 years old	3 Hello, how are you?	4 I am very well	5 I am so-so	6 Because I am tired (m)	7 What's your name?
15 My birthday is on	14 But I am nervous (f)	13 Because I am relaxed (f)	12 I am great	11 I am 12 years old	10 How old are you?	9 I am happy	8 I am a stressed (m)
16 the 20th of May	17 The 11th of June	18 When is your birthday?	19 I am not sad	20 I am bad	21 The 31st of October	22 I am 9 years old	23 Thank you
 ARRIVO	30 Good afternoon I am awful	29 I am cheerful (m)	28 I am 15 years old	27 The 30th of January	26 Because I am calm (f)	25 Good morning, I am so-so	24 The 26th of July

UNIT 5
IL MIO ANIMALE DOMESTICO

In this unit you will learn how to say in Italian:

- ✓ What pets you have at home
- ✓ What colour are your pets
- ✓ What their name is
- ✓ *Ho/ hai*
- ✓ *Non ho/ non hai*
- ✓ *Un/Una indefinite articles*

You will revisit:

- ★ Saying your name
- ★ How to say your age and birthday

Ho un cane

Ho un gatto

UNIT 5. IL MIO ANIMALE DOMESTICO
I can say what pets I have

Hai un animale in casa? *Do you have a pet at home?*

Io *I*	**ho** *I have* **non ho** *I do not have*	**un** *a*	**cane** *dog* **cavallo** *horse* **coniglio** *rabbit* **criceto** *hamster* **gatto** *cat* **pappagallo** *parrot* **pesce** *fish* **pinguino** *penguin* **porcellino d'India** *guinea pig* **ragno** *spider* **topo** *mouse* **uccellino** *bird*	**azzurro** *light blue* **bianco** *white* **giallo** *yellow* **grigio** *grey* **nero** *black* **piccolo** *small* **rosso** *red* **blu** *blue* **grande** *big* **marrone** *brown* **rosa** *pink* **verde** *green*	**che si chiama** *which is called* **e** *and* **però** *but*	**Coco** **Dida** **Lola** **Maia** **Paolo** **Pepe** **Rocky** **Zar**
Tu *You*	**hai** *you have* **non hai** *you do not have*	**una** *a*	**gallina** *chicken* **pecora** *sheep* **tartaruga** *tortoise/turtle*	**azzurra** **bianca** **gialla** **grigia** **nera** **piccola** **rossa**		

Io ho un gatto <u>e</u> un topo	*I have a cat and a mouse*
Tu hai un cane <u>però</u> non hai un gato	*You have a dog but you don't have a cat*
Non ho animali	*I don't have pets* 

Unit 5. I can say what pets I have: LISTENING 

1. Listen and complete with the missing vowel

a. Un c__ne

b. Un cav__llo

c. Un gatt__

d. Un p_sce

e. Una tortar__ga

f. Una pec__ra

g. Un con__glio

h. Una gall__na

a e i o u

2. Listen and tick the word you hear

	1	2	3
a.	un pesce	un uccellino	un coniglio
b.	un animale	una gallina	una pecora
c.	un cavallo	un topo	un gatto
d.	un pinguino	un cane	un pesce
e.	una pecora?	una tartaruga?	Un animale?

3. Complete with the missing letters in the box below

a. Un cane ne _ _ .

b. Una _ _ llina bianca.

c. Un ca _ _ llo grigio.

d. Un pesce azz _ _ _ _ _.

e. Un coni _ _ _ _ marrone.

f. Una pe _ _ ra nera.

g. Una tartaruga ro _ _ _ _.

h. Un pappagallo gia _ _ _ _ .

| glio | ga | llo | co | ro | ssa | urro | va |

THE LANGUAGE GYM

4. Complete the words with the missing endings

a. Un pesc__ giall__.

b. Una pecor__ ros__.

c. Un pappagall__ ross__.

d. Un gatt__ ner__.

e. Una tartarug__ marron__.

f. Un can__ bianc__.

g. Un pinguin__ piccol__.

h. Una gallin__ ner__.

i. Un pesc__ verd__.

j. Un porcellin__ d'Indi__ bianc__.

5. Write the missing word as you hear it

a. Un ______________ azzurro.

b. Una ______________ gialla.

c. Un ______________ rosa.

d. Un ______________ nero.

e. Una ______________ bianca.

f. Una ______________ rossa.

g. Un cane ___________.

h. Un topo ___________.

i. Una ______________ grande.

j. Ho un ______________.

k. _______ ho un gatto.

6. Faulty Echo

Underline the wrong word

a. Non ho un pinguino grigio.

b. Ho una pecora rosa.

c. Non hai un pesce azzurro.

d. Non ho un gatto piccolo.

e. Hai una gallina piccola.

f. Non hai un cavallo marrone.

g. Non ho animali.

h. Ho una tartaruga verde.

i. Ho un pappagallo giallo.

j. Non ho una gallina rossa.

7. Listen and choose the correct spelling

	1	2
a.	Mi ciamo	Mi chiamo
b.	Anni	Ani
c.	Pero	Però
d.	Coniglo	Coniglio
e.	Spaniolo	Spagnolo
f.	Cinque	Cinqe
g.	Giallo	Gialo
h.	Osso	Otto
i.	Patrizia	Patrisia
j.	Cavalo	Cavallo
k.	Pecora	Picora
l.	Aranchone	Arancione

8. Fill in the grid with the correct information in English

	Animale	Colore
a.		
b.		
c.		
d.		
e.		
f.		

9. Spot the Intruder
Identify the word in each sentence the speaker is NOT saying

    a. Ho un pesce azzurro e un due gatto grigio.

    b. Hai un animale? No, non ho un animali.

    c. Hai un cavallo bianco che come si chiama Rocky.

    d. Io ho un cane marrone e no grande.

    e. Tu non hai una pecora grande, però hai un topo piccolo.

    f. Io ho un pinguino bianco e nero nera che si chiama Pepe.

    g. Ho un gatto bianco bianca che si chiama Cat.

    h. Ho un pappagallo che si chiama chiamo Poppy.

10. Catch it, Swap it
Listen, spot the difference between what you hear and the written text and edit each sentence accordingly

e.g. *Ho un <u>gatto</u> marrone e bianco.* | *coniglio*

    a. Hai un cavallo grande e grigio.

    b. Non ho una pecora nera e gialla.

    c. Ho un coniglio, però non ho una pecora.

    d. Non hai un pesce azzurro, però hai una tartaruga.

    e. Hai un animale? Sí, ho un cane nero.

    f. Non ho un pinguino, però ho un pappagallo.

    g. Ho un uccellino piccolo che si chiama Rocky.

11. Listening Slalom

Listen and pick the equivalent English words from each column – drawing a line as you follow the speaker

e.g. ho un gatto nero – I have a black cat

You could colour in the boxes for each sentence in a different colour and read out the sentence in Italian

e.g.	*I have*		Light blue
a.	You have		*black*
b.	I don't have		pink
c.	I have		white
d.	You do not have		brown
e.	I have		grey
f.	I don't have		yellow

Unit 5. I can say what pets I have: READING

1. Sylla-Bees
Read and put the syllables in the cells in the correct order

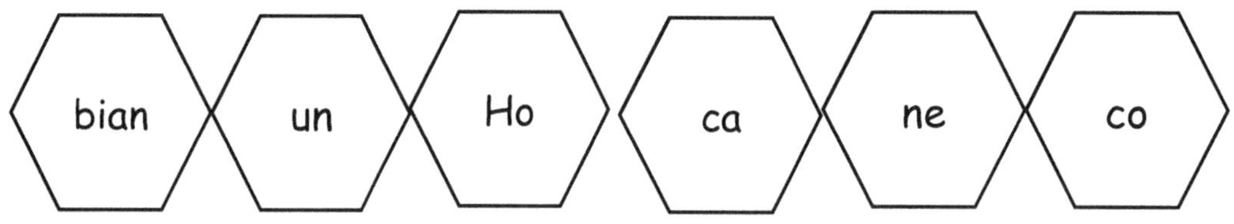

a. *I have a white dog:* H___________ u___ c________ b________.

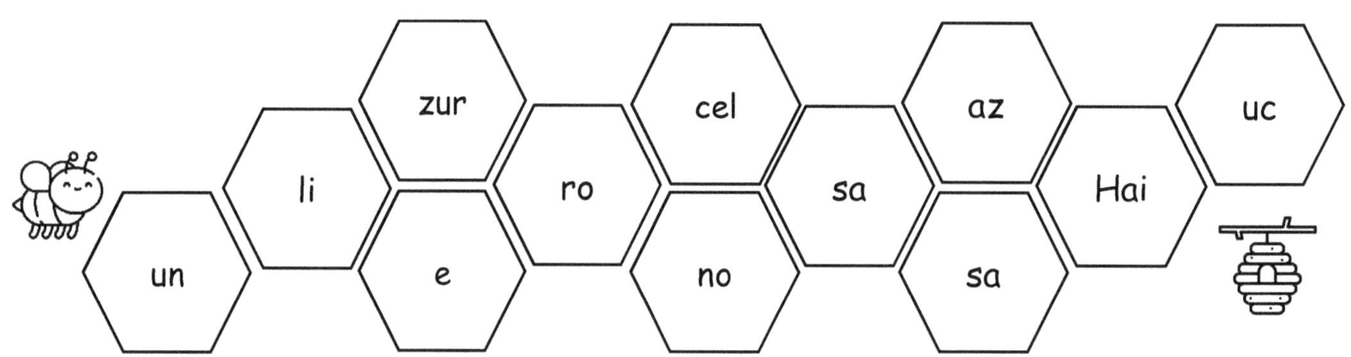

b. *You have a light blue and pink bird:* H____u____u___________
a________ e r_________.

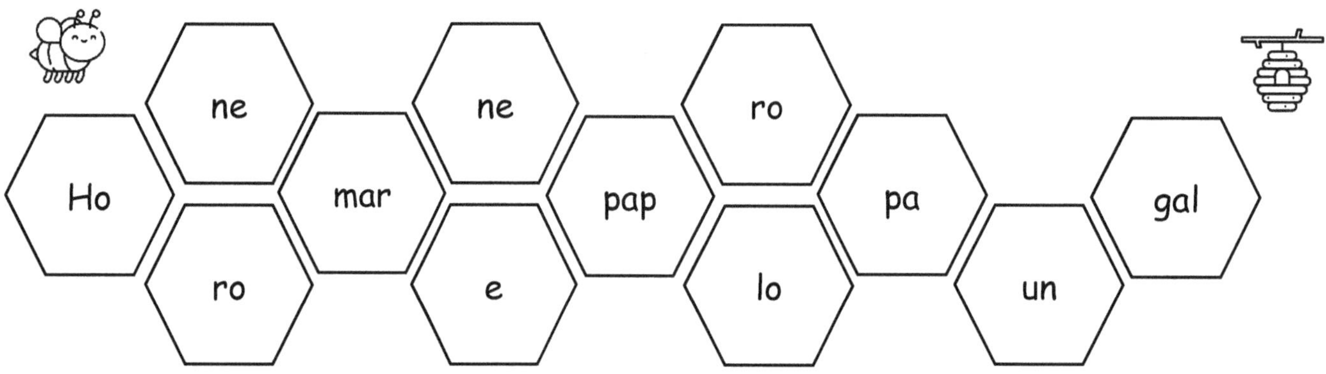

c. *I have a brown and black parrot:* H_____ u___ p___________
m___________ e n__________.

THE LANGUAGE GYM

2. Read, Match, Find and Colour

A. Match these sentences to the pictures above. 1 is odd.

a. Ho un coniglio grigio e rosa.
b. Hai una tartaruga verde e rossa.
c. Ho un pinguino bianco e nero.
d. Non ho una gallina bianca.
e. Ho un pesce azzurro e giallo.
f. Ho un cane marrone e grigio.
g. Hai un gatto piccolo.
h. Non hai una pecora bianca e rosa.
i. Ho un topo nero, rosso e verde .
j. Ho un cavallo grande.
k. Non ho animali.

B. Using the sentences in task A find the Italian for:

a. A white chicken.
b. I have a fish.
c. A white sheep.
d. A green turtle.
e. Brown and grey.
f. A small cat.
g. A big horse.
h. I have a penguin.
i. You do not have.
j. I do not have.
k. I don't have pets.

3. True or False
Read the paragraphs below and then answer True or False

		True	False
1	**a. Enrico** is 10 years old.		
	b. His birthday is on the 4th July.		
	c. He has a grey dog.		
	d. His pet is called Zagor.		
	e. He has a white horse.		
2	**a. Carlotta** is 7 years old.		
	b. Her birthday is on the 3rd March.		
	c. She has a white cat.		
	d. Her cat is called Lola.		
	e. She has a black cat.		

4. Tick or Cross

A. Read the text. Tick the box if you find the words in the text, cross it if you do not find them.

- Ciao, mi chiamo **Stefano.**

Ho undici anni. Il mio compleanno é il diciannove gennaio. Ho un gatto rosso e bianco che si chiama Romolo. È un gatto grande. ¿Tu hai animali?

- Ciao, mi chiamo **Beatrice**

Ho sette anni. Il mio compleanno é il dodici aprile. Ho un coniglio nero e bianco che si chiama Cocco. È un coniglio piccolo.

	✓	✗
a. Mi chiamo		
b. Tredici anni		
c. Un gatto grande		
d. Un coniglio		
e. Un cane grigio		
f. Che si chiama		

g. I am 7 years old		
h. My birthday		
i. Black and brown		
j. Black and white		
k. I have a cat		
l. Small rabbit		

B. Find the Italian in the texts above

a. My name is _______________________________________

b. My birthday is _______________________________________

c. It is a big cat. _______________________________________

d. Do you have pets? _______________________________________

e. I have a black rabbit. _______________________________________

5. Language Detective

- <u>Mi chiamo</u> **Carlo.** Ho dodici anni. Il mio compleanno é il quindici febbraio. Ho un pappagallo giallo che si chiama Paolo, però non ho un cane nero.

- Mi chiamo **Maria.** Ho tredici anni. Il mio compleanno é il venti gennaio. Ho un topo grigio che si chiama Zar, però non ho un pesce azzurro.

- Ciao, Mi chiamo **Manuele.** Ho sei anni. Il mio compleanno é il due giugno. Ho un pappagallo verde che si chiama Coco, però non ho un cavallo bianco.

- Buongiorno, mi chiamo **Mia.** Ho undici anni. Il mio compleanno é il quattordici maggio. Ho una pecora marrone e bianca che si chiama Pia .

A. Find someone who…

a. …is 12 years old

b. …has a green parrot

c. …has a grey mouse

d. …was born on the 2nd June

e. …does not have a black dog

f. …was born in January

g. …has a sheep

h. …is 11 years old

B. Put a cross in the box and underline the corresponding Italian translation. One is odd.

My name is	a yellow parrot	brown and white
I have a sheep	My birthday	I am 8 years old
which is called	I don't have	15th of February
a black dog	14th of May	but I don't have

Unit 5. I can say what pets I have: WRITING

1. Spelling

a. H__   *I have*

b. U__ g__ __ __ __   *A cat*

c. __n c__ __ __ ll __   *A horse*

d. Un c__ __ e m__ __ __ o __ __   *A brown dog*

e. Un t__ __ __ g__ __ llo   *A yellow mouse*

f. H__ __   *You have*

g. U__ a__ __ __ __ __ __   *A pet*

2. Anagrams: unscramble the Italian

a. oH un nace rnoe.   *I have a black dog.*

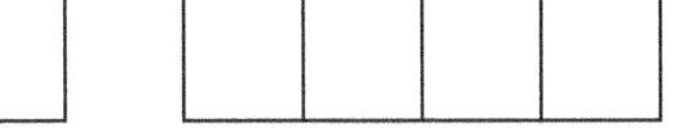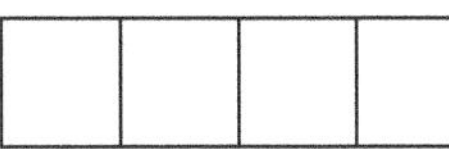

b. noN oh nu otagt derve.   *I do not have a green cat.*

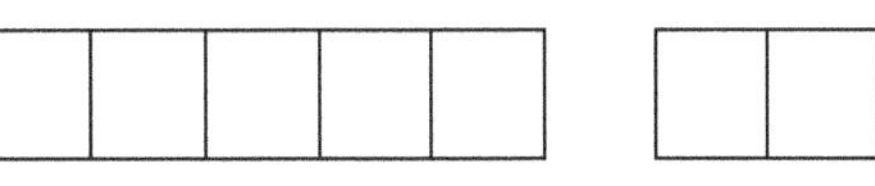

c. oH nua ocraep ramoren.   *I have a brown sheep.*

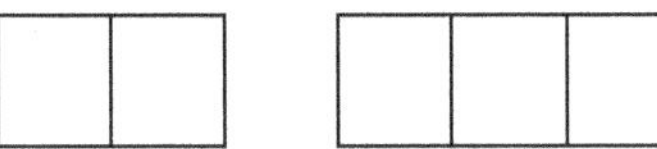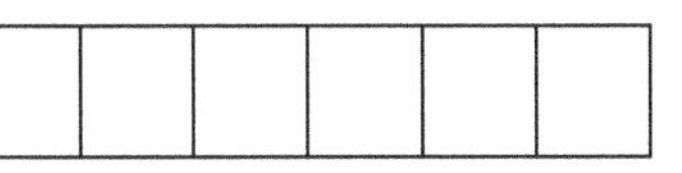

d. oH anu grattaura sarso.   *I have a red turtle.*

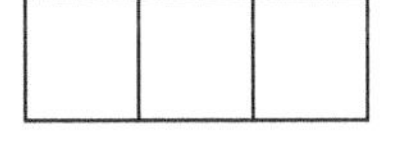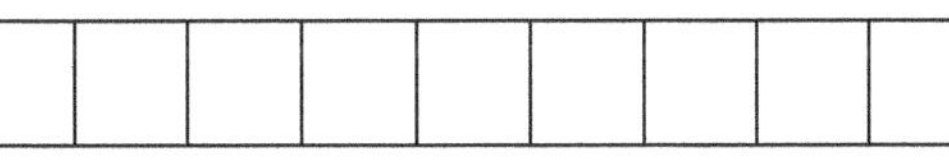

e. oH nu opto rurzazo.   *I have a light blue mouse.*

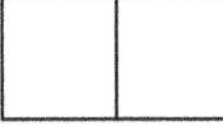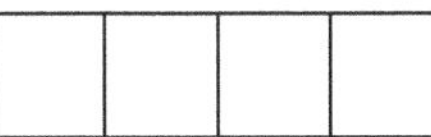

THE LANGUAGE GYM

3. Gapped Translation

a. Ho sette anni.

I am ___________ years old.

b. Ho un gatto piccolo.

I have a ____________ cat.

c. Non ho un ragno.

I do not have a __________.

d. Tu hai un cavallo marrone.

___ have a brown _______.

e. Ho una pecora che si chiama Dida.

I have a sheep ________ Dida.

f. Ho un cavallo bianco.

I ______ a white _________.

g. Hai animali?

Do _____ _______ pets?

h. Non ho animali.

I do not have _________.

i. Ho una tartaruga nera.

I have a black ____________.

4. Split Sentences

a. Ho un

b. Una tartaruga

c. Ho

d. Ho una

e. Un cavallo

f. Non

g. Hai

1. bianca

2. gatto

3. un uccellino

4. nero

5. ho animali

6. un animale?

7. gallina

a	b	c	d	e	f	g
2						

5. Rock Climbing

Starting from the bottom, pick one chunk from each row to translate the sentences in the grid below.

a.	b.	c.	d.	e.
e rosa.	nero.	Rocky.	bianca.	e marrone.
piccola	gallina	grande	chiama	gatto
un	si	una	una tartaruga	un cavallo
Il mio cane	Ho	Non ho	Hai	Non hai

a.	*My dog is called Rocky.*

b.	*I have a white chicken.*

c.	*I don't have a black cat.*

d.	*You have a big and brown horse.*

e.	*You do not have a small and pink turtle.*

6. Mosaic Translation

Use the words in the grid to help you translate the sentences below.

a.	Ho	un gatto	Luce	ho	Dida.
b.	Non ho	tartaruga	nero	e	un pappagallo.
c.	La mia gallina	un pinguino	piccola	ed è	marrone.
d.	Il mio cane	si chiama	grande	nero e	bianco.
e.	Ho una	è	però	che si chiama	bianca.

a. *I have a black and white penguin.*

____

b. *I don't have a cat but I have a parrot.*

____

c. *My chicken is called Luce and it is white.*

____

d. *My dog is big, black and brown.*

____

e. *I have a small tortoise which is called Dida.*

____

7. Sentence Puzzle

Put the words in the correct order

a. Ho cane Marrone un. _______________________________

b. un Hai animale? _______________________________

c. un pappagallo Hai. _______________________________

d. Ho gatto bianco un. _______________________________

e. gallina Ho una piccola. _______________________________

f. un azzurro pesce Hai giallo e. _______________________________

g. Ho bianca tartaruga una. _______________________________

h. ho animali Non. _______________________________

i. gatto Ho e bianco nero un. _______________________________

8. Tangled Translation

a. Write the Italian words in English to complete the translation

Hello, **mi chiamo** Davide. I am **sette anni. Il mio compleanno** is on the **diciotto**

July. **Ho un** white dog **che si chiama** Lily. **É molto** big.

b. Write the English words in Italian to complete the translation

Hello, mi chiamo Gianfranco. **I am** nove **years old.** Il mio **birthday** é il venti **of**

June. **I have a blue fish** che si chiama Nemo. É molto **small.**

9. Fill in the Gaps

a. Ciao, mi ___________ Enrico e ho dieci anni. Il mio compleanno é il

_________ giugno. _________ un cavallo _______ che si ______ Zar.

chiamo	Ho	cinque	grigio	chiama

b. Ciao, mi chiamo Carlo. Ho __________ anni. Il mio compleanno é il

 diciannove _________. Ho un _________ marrone e _______ che si

chiama Tobia . É _____________.

piccolo	cane	bianco	gennaio	undici

10. Guided Translation

a. M__ ch_______ S__________ e h______ u______ a________.
My name is Stefano and I am 11 years old.

b. H______ u__ c________ g______ c___ s__ c______ P_____.
I have a grey rabbit, which is called Pepe.

c. N__ h______ u__ p_________, p_______ h___ u__ g________.
I do not have a parrot, but I have a chicken.

d. H_______ u___ c_______ m________ e u___ g______ n______.
You have a brown dog and a black cat.

e. N__ h____ u___ t_________, p___ h______ u___ r______.
You do not have a tortoise, but you have a spider.

f. N___ h________ u___ p_________ b____________.
I do not have a white sheep.

11. Pyramid Translation

Starting from the top, translate chunks into Italian. Write the sentences in the box below.

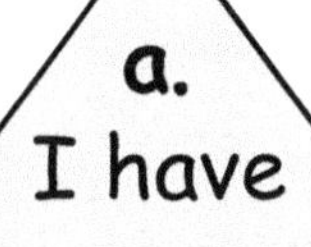

a.
I have

b. I have a white bird

c. I have a white bird which is called Doria

d. I have a white bird which is called Doria, but I do not have...

e. I have a white bird which is called Doria, but I do not have a black tortoise.

a.

b.

c.

d.

e.

THE LANGUAGE GYM

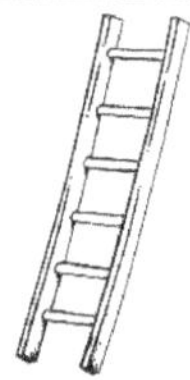

12. Staircase Translation

Starting from the top, translate each chunk into Italian.
Write the sentences in the grid below.

a.	Do you have	a dog?				
b.	I do not have	a white	sheep.			
c.	You have	a black	horse	which is called Zar.		
d.	I have	a brown	cat	and	a big tortoise.	
e.	I have	a small fish	and	you have	a grey	penguin.

Answers / Risposte

a.	
b.	
c.	
d.	
e.	

Challenge / Sfida

Can you create 2 more sentences using the words in the staircase grid?

☆	
☆	

UNIT 6
NEL MIO ZAINO

In this unit you will learn how to say in Italian:

- ✓ What items you have in your pencil case/school bag
- ✓ What colour are your school items

You will revisit:
- ★ How to use *ho/hai*
- ★ *C'è/non c'è*
- ★ Indefinite articles *un/una*
- ★ Word order noun + adjective

Ho un astuccio bianco

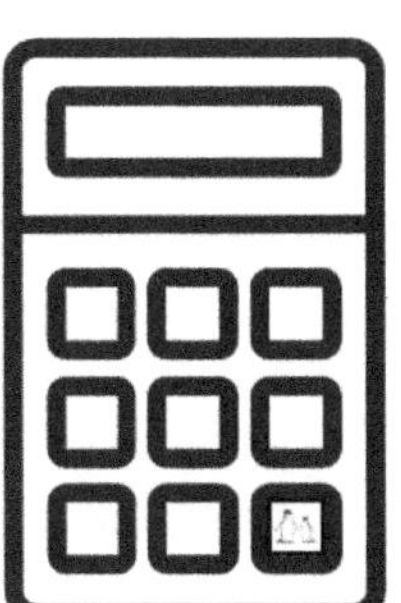

Ho una calcolatrice rossa

69

UNIT 6. NEL MIO ZAINO
I can say what's in my schoolbag

> **Cosa hai nel tuo zaino?** *What do you have in your schoolbag?*
> **Cosa c'è nel tuo astuccio?** *What's in your pencil case?*

Nel mio zaino *In my schoolbag*	ho *I have* / c'è *there is*	un *a*	astuccio *pencil case* diario *planner* libro *book* pennarello *felt-tip pen* quaderno *exercise book* temperamatite *pencil sharpener*	arancione *orange* azzurro *blue* bianco *white* giallo *yellow* grigio *grey* marrone *brown* nero *black* rosso *red* rosa *pink* verde *green*
		uno *a*	*zaino *a schoolbag*	
Nel mio astuccio *In my pencil case*	non ho *I have not* / non c'è *there is not*	una *a*	calcolatrice *calculator* cartella *folder* colla *glue* gomma *rubber* matita *pencil* matita colorata *coloured pencil* penna *pen* riga *ruler*	arancione azzurra bianca gialla grigia marrone nera rossa rosa verde

Author's note:

1) *We know you won't have a schoolbag IN your schoolbag! But take note that because zaino starts with a "z", we must say "uno" zaino *a schoolbag.*

2) To say you have two or more things in your bag or pencil case, we say "ci sono" *(there are).* e.g. Nel mio zaino <u>ci sono</u> un libro e una cartella.

Unit 6. I can say what's in my schoolbag: LISTENING

1. Faulty Echo

e.g. nel mio zaino ho un libro.

a. Nel mio astuccio c'è una colla

b. Cos' hai nel tuo zaino?

c. Nel mio zaino ho una calcolatrice.

d. Nel mio astuccio ho una riga.

e. Nel mio zaino c'è un quaderno.

f. Ho una gomma e una penna.

2. Listen and Match

a.   **1.** 

b.   **2.** 

c.   **3.** 

d.   **4.** 

e.   **5.** 

f.   **6.** 

3. Listen and tick the word you hear

	1	2	3
e.g.	*Cartella*	*Calcolatrice*	*Cartella* ✓
a.	Zaino	Penna	Matita
b.	Diario	Astuccio	Libro
c.	Matita	Temperamatite	Matita colorata
d.	Ho	Gomma	C'è
e.	Colla	C'è	Non c'è

4. Fill in the grid with the correct information in English

		Item	Colour
e.g.	Ivano	Calculator	Red
a.	Liliana		
b.	Mario		
c.	Dario		
d.	Valentina		

5. Listen and complete with the missing vowels

a. Una calc__latric__.

b. Un l__bro azz__rro.

c. Un t__mp__ramatite.

d. Una cart__lla.

e. Uno za__no.

f. Una p__nn__ ner__.

g. Una cart__lla ross__.

h. Un p__nnarello giall__.

i. Un__ zaino v__rde.

j. Una mat__ta color_ta r__sa.

a
e
i
o
u

6. Complete with the missing syllables in the box below

a. Una _ _ _ la gialla.

b. Una _ _ tita colorata verde.

c. Un _ _ _ rio rosso.

d. Una ma _ _ ta nera.

e. Un a _ _ _ _ cio giallo.

f. Uno za _ no bianco.

g. Ho un temperamatite ros _ _.

h. Una cal _ _ latrice nera.

i. Cosa _ _ i nel tuo astuccio?

j. Una car _ _ _ la arancione.

dia	stuc	so	tel	ma	col	ti	co	i	ha

7. Break the flow: Draw a line between words

a. Nelmioastuccioc'èunpennarellogrigio.

b. Nelmiozainoc'èunlibro.

c. Nelmiozainohoundiarioazzurro.

d. Nelmioastucciohounagommabianca.

e. Nelmiozainoc'èunacalcolatricenera.

f. Cosahaineltuozaino?Hounacartellamarrone.

g. Cosac'èneltuoastuccio?C'èunapennarossa.

h. Hounamatitaperònonhounariga.

8. Spot the Intruder

Identify the words in each sentence the speaker is NOT saying

a. Nel mio astuccio non c'è una matita azzurra

b. Nel mio astuccio ho c'è una gomma e una colla.

c. Nel mio astuccio ci sono una gomma, un temperamatite e una riga.

d. Cos' hai nel tuo un astuccio?

e. Cosa ho c'è nel tuo zaino?

f. Nel mio zaino non ho una calcolatrice gialla e verde.

g. Nel mio zaino ci sono una matita, un libro e un quaderno rosso.

9. Catch it, Swap it

Listen, spot the difference between what you hear and the written text and edit each sentence accordingly.

e.g. Nel mio <u>zaino</u> ho una gomma.

a. Nel mio zaino ho una colla verde.

b. Nel mio astuccio c'è un pennarello nero.

c. Nel mio zaino c'è una calcolatrice rosa.

d. Nel mio zaino non ho una cartella azzurra.

e. Nel mio astuccio non c'è un temperamatite giallo.

f. Nel mio zaino non c'è una penna rossa.

g. Non ho un quaderno rosso.

astuccio

10. Sentence bingo

Write 4 of the sentences into the grid. You will hear sentences in Italian in a RANDOM ORDER. Tick all 4 of your sentences to win bingo.

1. Nel mio zaino non c'è un libro giallo.
2. Nel mio zaino ho una colla verde.
3. Nel mio astuccio ho un pennarello.
4. Nel mio zaino ho un pennarello.
5. Nel mio zaino ho un diario nero.
6. Nel mio astuccio c'è una calcolatrice rosa.
7. Non ho una matita verde.
8. Nel mio zaino non ho una matita azzurra.
9. Nel mio zaino non c'è una cartella rossa.
10. Non ho un quaderno rosso.

11. Listening Slalom

Listen and pick the equivalent English words from each column
e.g. *ho una matita grigia e una gomma.*

Word Order Alert!

As you have seen already, colours (and other adjectives) follow the noun in Italian.
In this exercise you will hear: **Ho** (I have) **una matita** (a pencil) **grigia** (grey).

e.g.	*I have*	there are	a pencil sharpener	but there is a ruler.
a.	In my pencil case	*a grey*	a black pen	*and a rubber.* 
b.	In my schoolbag	I have	*pencil*	and a red folder.
c.	In my pencil case	there isn't	a blue book	and a calculator.
d.	I don't have	I have	a yellow ruler	a red notebook
e.	In my pencil case	I have an orange	I have	and a pink pencil.
f.	In my schoolbag	a white rubber but	folder but I don't have	a glue.

Challenge / Sfida

Can you read the sentences in Italian? You could use a colour/pattern to identify the
4 chunks of each sentence!

Unit 6. I can say what's in my schoolbag: READING

1. Sylla-bees.
Read and put the syllables in the cells in the correct order

ti | tem | un | ho | ra | Io | pe | ma | te

a. *I have a pencil sharpener.*
I______ h______ u____ t________________.

una | mio | cio | ho
stuc | ca | a | ma
bian | Nel | gom

b. *In my pencil case I have a white rubber.*
N__ m__ a__________ h___ u___ g______ b________.

Nel | no | una | a | é
i | zur | za | rio | c
di | az | ro | mio

c. *In my schoolbag there is a blue planner.*
N__ m__ z__________ c' è u_____ d__________ a________.

2. Read, Match, Find and Colour

A. Match these sentences to the pictures above:

a. Nel mio astuccio ho una matita grigia.

b. Ho uno zaino rosso e nero.

c. Nel mio astuccio c'è una gomma bianca.

d. Hai una calcolatrice?

e. Ho una penna verde.

f. Nel mio zaino c'è un libro giallo.

g. Ho un temperamatite azzurro.

h. Nel mio astuccio c'è una riga rosa.

i. Non ho un diario arancione.

j. Nel mio zaino ho una cartella.

B. Using the sentences in task A find the Italian for:

a. A blue pencil sharpener.

b. I have a school bag.

c. In my pencil case.

d. There is a ruler.

e. A pink ruler.

f. I do not have.

g. I have a folder.

h. Red and black.

i. You have.

j. An orange diary.

3. True or False

A. Read the paragraphs below and then answer True or False

	True	False
a. **Paolo** is 11 years old.		
b. His birthday is on the 13th July.		
c. He has a dog and a cat.		
d. In his schoolbag there is a book.		
e. He has a pink folder.		
f. He does not have a ruler.		
g. **Anna** is 10 years old.		
h. She has a dog but does not have a horse.		
i. In her pencil case she has a blue pen.		
j. She does not have a sharpener.		

B. Find in the texts above the Italian for:

a. My birthday is

b. In my schoolbag

c. I have a rabbit

d. A yellow workbook

e. I don't have a sharpener

f. An orange rubber

4. Tick or Cross

A. Read the texts. Tick the box if you find the words in the text, cross it if you do not find them.

Ciao, mi chiamo **Maria.**

Ho tredici anni. Il mio compleanno é il quindici febbraio. Ho un pesce che si chiama Ricky. Nel mio zaino c'è una calcolatrice, una cartella gialla e una colla, però non c'è un diario rosa.

Ciao, mi chiamo **Giovanni.**

Ho otto anni. Il mio compleanno é il sei luglio. Ho un coniglio, però non ho una tartaruga. Nel mio astuccio ho un temperamatite, una matita e una riga bianca, però non ho una gomma.

	✓	✗
a. Ho tredici anni.		
b. Il dodici...		
c. Nel mio astuccio.		
d. Una calcolatrice.		
e. Una colla.		
f. Però non c'è...		

g. I am 9 years old.		
h. The 7th of June.		
i. But I don't have...		
j. In my pencil case.		
k. A pencil.		
l. And a ruler.		

B. Find the Italian in the texts above

a. The 15th of February. _______________________________________

b. In my schoolbag. _______________________________________

c. A pink diary. _______________________________________

d. A white ruler. _______________________________________

e. I do not have a rubber. _______________________________________

5. Language detective

- Mi chiamo **Riccardo.** Ho dieci anni. Il mio compleanno é il cinque marzo. Ho un cavallo marrone. Nel mio zaino ho un diario rosso <u>e un libro,</u> però non ho una cartella bianca.

- Mi chiamo **Marta.** Ho quattordici anni. Il mio compleanno é il ventiquattro maggio. Ho un gatto piccolo. Nel mio astuccio ho una calcolatrice e un quaderno verde, però non ho un pennarello giallo.

- Ciao, sono **Enea.** Ho undici anni. Il mio compleanno é il trenta aprile. Ho una tartaruga grande. Nel mio zaino c'è una riga gialla e una penna nera, però non c'è un temperamatite grigio.

A. Find someone who...

a. ...is 14 years old

b. ...has a red diary

c. ...has a green exercise book

d. ...has a yellow ruler

e. ...does not have a white folder

f. ...has a black pen

g. ...is 10 years old

B. Put a cross in the box and underline the corresponding Italian translation. One is odd.

And a book	A big tortoise	The 30th of April
A green notebook	A brown horse	I am 11 years old
A grey sharpener	But there is not	In my school bag
In my pencil case	A yellow glue	But I do not have

1. Spelling

a. U__ __ r__ __ __   A ruler

b. U__ __i __ __ __   A book

c. __n__ __ __ __ __ __ __ a   A pencil

d. Un t__ __ __ __ r __ __ __ __ __ __ __ __   A pencil sharpener

e. Un __ __ a __ __ __   A diary

f. __ n __ __ __ i __ __   A schoolbag

g. __ n p__ __ __ a __ __ __ __ __   A felt-tip pen

2. Anagrams: unscramble the Italian

a. oH uan rgai canbia.   *I have a white ruler.*

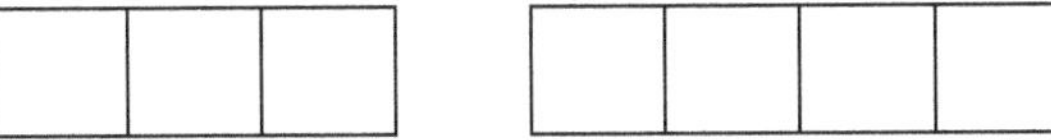

b. iaH aun ommga rena.   *You have a black rubber.*

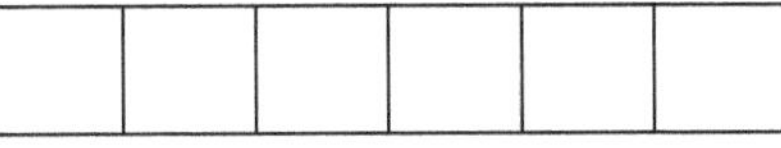

c. onN ho nu brilo.   *I don't have a book.*

d. iHa nua tamita saros.   *You have a red pencil.*

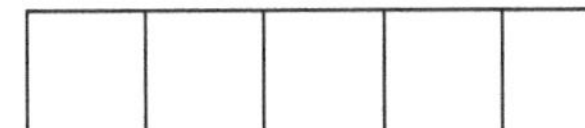

THE LANGUAGE GYM

3. Gapped Translation

a. Ho una matita arancione e una colla.

   I have an _______________ pencil and a _________ .

b. Nel mio astuccio c'è una penna verde e una riga.

   In my pencil case there is a green ____________ and a _________.

c. Non ho un temperamatite, peró ho una gomma.

   I do not have a __________________, but I have a ____________.

d. Cosa hai nel tuo zaino? Ho un libro.

   _______ do you ________ in your ___________? I have a _________.

4. Split Sentences

a. Ho un	**1.** una matita.
b. Nel mio zaino	**2.** temperamatite azzurro.
c. Ho una	**3.** ho un libro.
d. Non ho	**4.** nel tuo astuccio?
e. Nel mio astuccio c'è	**5.** un quaderno verde.
f. Cosa hai	**6.** nera.
g. Non c'è una penna	**7.** cartella rosa.

1	
2	
3	
4	
5	
6	
7	

5. Rock Climbing

Starting from the bottom, pick one chunk from each row to translate the sentences below.

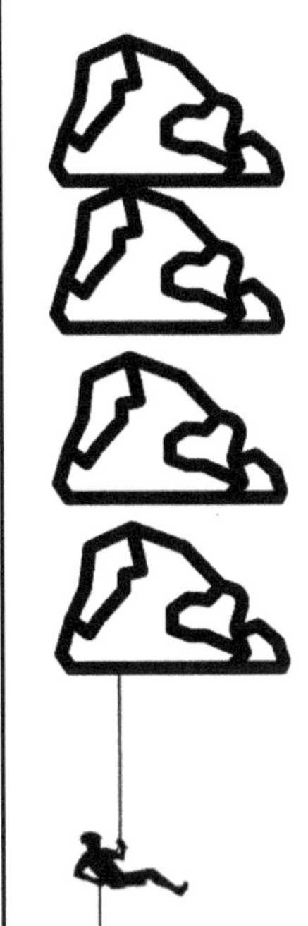

a.	b.	c.	d.	e.
un diario rosso.	una cartella.	una riga.	penna.	grigia.
e una matita	un libro e	ho una	però ho	però non ho
una colla	astuccio	una gomma gialla	temperamatite	c'è
Nel mio	Non ho	Hai	Nel mio zaino	Ho un

a. In my pencil case I have a pen.

____

b. I do not have a glue stick, but I have a folder.

____

c. You have a yellow rubber and a grey pencil.

____

d. In my schoolbag there is a book and a red diary.

____

e. I have a sharpener, but I do not have a ruler.

____

6. Mosaic Translation
Use the words in the grid to help you translate the sentences below.

a.	Nel mio	un pennarello	calcolatrice	ho un	gomma rosa.
b.	Ho una	zaino	nera	e una matita	astuccio.
c.	Nel mio astuccio	hai	azzurra	e una	libro rosso.
d.	Cosa	penna	nel tuo zaino?	nel mio	arancione.
e.	Non c'è	Ho un	c'è una	cartella	verde.

a. *In my schoolbag there is an orange folder.*

____

b. *I have a blue pen and a green pencil.*

____

c. *In my pencil case I have a pencil sharpener and a pink rubber.*

____

d. *What do you have in your schoolbag? I have a red book.*

____

e. *There isn't a black calculator in my pencil case.*

____

7. Sentence Puzzle
Put the words in the correct order

a. zaino Nel libro ho mio un verde

In my schoolbag I have a green book.

b. nel tuo hai Cosa astuccio?

What do you have in your pencil case?

c. Nel una riga c'è gialla mio astuccio

In my pencil case there is a yellow ruler.

d. però non un temperamatite c'è Nel astuccio mio gomma una c'è

In my pencil case there is a sharpener, but there isn't a rubber.

8. Tangled Translation

a. Write the Italian words in English to complete the translation

Hello, **mi chiamo** Gianni. **Ho** nine years old. My birthday **é il ventisei** of January. I have **un cane** brown **che si chiama Michele.** In my pencil case there is **una gomma bianca e** a red ruler, but **non c'è** a **temperamatite** grey.

b. Write the English words in Italian to complete the translation

Buongiorno, **my name is** Emma. **I am** tredici anni. Il mio compleanno **is on the 15th** febbraio. Ho **a horse** nero che si chiama Bandito. **In my schoolbag there is** un libro verde e **a yellow exercise book,** però non c'è **a pink folder.**

9. Fill in the gaps

a. Ciao, mi chiamo Luciano e _________ undici anni. Il mio compleanno é ____ venti giugno. Nel mio __________ ho una __________ , una penna e ________ gomma __________.

| una | matita | ho | il | astuccio | bianca |

b. Ciao, _____ chiamo Carmela. Ho un ________ grigio. Nel mio zaino ______ un libro, un _____________ e un quaderno _____________. Però non c'è una_____________.

| temperamatite | c'è | cartella | mi | giallo | coniglio |

10. Guided Translation

a. N__ m__ z_________ c'___ u___ d________ a_________.

In my schoolbag there is an orange diary.

b. N__ m__ a________ h__ u___ m________ a_______.

In my pencil case I have a blue pencil.

c. N__ c'_____ u___ g______ n__ m___ a_____________.

There isn't a rubber in my pencil case.

d. N___ h______ u___ r______, p____ h___ u__ l______.

I don't have a ruler, but I have a book.

e. H__ u___ a_________ r______ n___ m__ z_________.

I have a red pencil case in my schoolbag.

11. Pyramid Translation

Starting from the top, translate each chunk in Italian. Write the sentences in the box below.

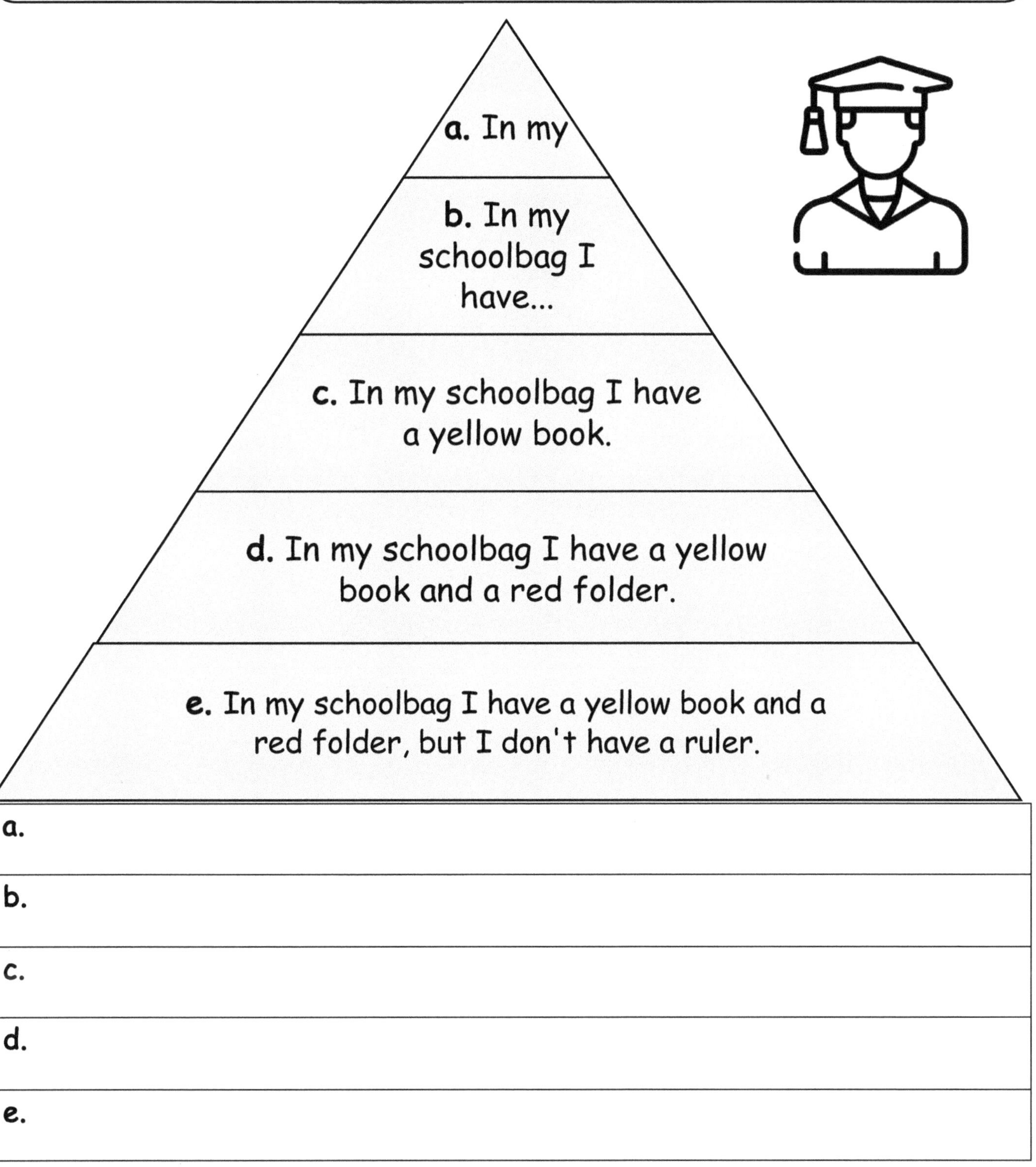

a.

b.

c.

d.

e.

THE LANGUAGE GYM

12. Staircase Translation

Starting from the top, translate each chunk into Italian.
Write the sentences in the grid below.

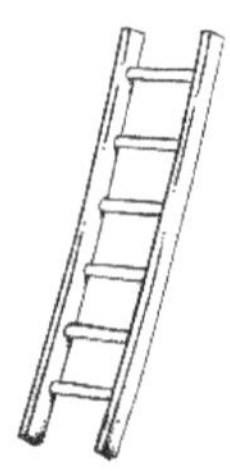

a.	I have a	red pen.				
b.	What	do you have	in your schoolbag?			
c.	In my pencil case	there is	a green pencil	and a ruler.		
d.	I don't have	a rubber	but	I have	a grey sharpener.	
e.	In my schoolbag	there isn't	a book	but there is	a calculator	and a diary.

Answers / Risposte

a.	
b.	
c.	
d.	
e.	

Challenge / Sfida

Can you create 2 more sentences using the words in the staircase grid above?

☆	
☆	

No Snakes No Ladders

THE LANGUAGE GYM

PARTENZA	1 Ho un gatto	2 Ho un cavallo	3 Ho una riga	4 Nel mio astuccio	5 Hai un animale?	6 Non ho animali	7 Una tartaruga verde
15 Un criceto marrone	14 Ho un astuccio verde	13 Un coniglio grande	12 Un temperamatite rosso	11 Un topo grigio	10 Non ho un pinguino	9 C'è una cartella	8 Una pecora bianca
16 Hai una tartaruga	17 Non ho una penna	18 Un cane nero	19 Nel mio zaino	20 Un pesce azzurro	21 Ho una gomma	22 Ho una matita	23 Che si chiama Pepe
ARRIVO	30 Hai una gallina piccola	29 Un uccellino giallo	28 Ho un quaderno arancione	27 Non ho una penna rosa	26 Non c'è un diario bianco	25 Non c'è una colla	24 C'è un libro azzurro

No Snakes No Ladders

 PARTENZA	1 I have a cat	2 I have a horse	3 I have a ruler	4 In my pencil case	5 Do you have a pet?	6 I don't have pets	7 A green tortoise
15 A brown hamster	14 I have a green pencil case	13 A big rabbit	12 A red pencil sharpener	11 A grey mouse	10 I don't have a penguin	9 There is a folder	8 A white sheep
16 You have a tortoise	17 I don't have a pen	18 A black dog	19 In my school bag	20 A blue fish	21 I have a rubber	22 I have a pencil	23 Which is called Pepe
ARRIVO	30 You have a small chicken	29 A yellow bird	28 I have an orange exercise book	27 I don't have a pink pen	26 There isn't a white planner	25 There isn't a glue	24 There is a blue book

UNIT 7
DI DOVE SEI?

In this unit you will learn how to:

- ✓ Say where you are from
- ✓ Say what languages you speak
- ✓ Use *sono/ non sono, sei/ non sei*
- ✓ *Parlo/non parlo, parli/non parli*
- ✓ Use some connectives
- ✓ Ask and understand what the weather is like

You will revisit:

- ★ Saying your age and birthday
- ★ Talking about your pets

Di dove sei?

Sono italiano/a

UNIT 7. DI DOVE SEI?
I can say where I am from and what languages I speak

> **Di dove sei?** *Where are you from?*
> **Quali lingue parli?** *What languages do you speak?*

	MASCULINE	FEMININE					
Sono *I am*	**americano** *American*	americana	**e** *and*	**parlo** *I speak*	**bene** *well*	**l'**	**inglese** *English*
	australiano *Australian*	australiana					**irlandese** *Irish*
	cinese *Chinese*	cinese	**però** *but*	**non parlo** *I don't speak*	**male** *bad*		**italiano** *Italian*
	francese *French*	francese				**lo**	**spagnolo** *Spanish*
	inglese *English*	inglese					**cinese** *Chinese*
	irlandese *Irish*	irlandese					**francese** *French*
	italiano *Italian*	italiana					**gallese** *Welsh*
	scozzese *Scottish*	scozzese				**il**	**portoghese** *Portuguese*
	spagnolo *Spanish*	spagnola					**tedesco** *German*
	tedesco *German*	tedesca					

Author's note: *Languages in Italian are all masculine and need the article.*
*Il is used with **masculine** words beginning with **most consonants**: **e.g.** il cinese*
*Lo is used with **masculine** words beginning with **z or s + consonant**: **e.g.** lo spagnolo*
*L' is used with **masculine** and **feminine** words beginning with a **vowel**: **e.g.** l'inglese*

Unit 7. Where I am from & languages I speak: LISTENING

1. Split sentences. Listen and match.

a. Sono	**1.** sei?
b. Parlo bene	**2.** gallese
c. Non sono	**3.** l'inglese
d. Non parlo bene	**4.** irlandese
e. Di dove	**5.** parli?
f. Parlo male	**6.** chiami?
g. Quali lingue	**7.** il francese
h. Come ti	**8.** il cinese

2. Faulty Echo.

e.g. *Sono <u>argentina.</u>*

a. Non sono cinese.

b. Sono spagnolo.

c. Parlo bene l'inglese.

d. Parlo male il tedesco.

e. Non parlo bene il francese.

f. Parlo bene italiano, però non parlo portoghese.

g. Non parlo bene l'inglese.

3. Listen and tick the word you hear

	1	2	3
a.	inglese	cinese	francese
b.	parlare	parli	parlo
c.	spagnola	spagnolo	scozzese
d.	francese	cinese	inglese
e.	tedesco	italiana	italiano

4. Fill in the grid with the correct information in English

		Nationality	Language
a.	Roberto		
b.	Francesca		
c.	Pamela		
d.	Ronaldo		

5. Listen and complete with the missing letters

a. S__no spag__o__a.

b. No__ son__ fran__ese.

c. Parlo be__e l'__nglese.

d. __rlo ben__ l__ spagn__lo.

e. P__rlo m__le __l tedes__o.

f. Parl__ cin__se? No, parlo ga__lese.

g. Sono scoz__ese e parlo ben__ il francese.

h. Parl__ bene l'ir__andese per__ male l'italian__.

i. So__o gall__se __ parlo bene il portoghe__e.

j. Parl__ bene italiano? S__, parl__ bene l'italiano.

6. Complete with the missing syllables in the box below

a. _ _ _ lo bene il _ _nese.

b. Parlo male _ _ tede_ _ _.

c. So_ _ in_ _ _se.

d. Parlo bene porto_ _ _se.

e. Parlo male il _ _ _lese.

f. _ _ _ _ parlo bene lo spa_ _ _lo.

g. Sono ameri_ _na e parlo bene il ci_ _se.

h. Sono fran_ _se _ _rò non parlo bene l'italiano.

i. Sono _ _ _toghese e parlo bene _ _ spagnolo.

j. Sono australia_ _ e parlo bene l'ita_ _ _no.

k. Sono tede_ _ _ e parlo bene an_ _ _ l'inglese.

l. Sono spagno_ _ e parlo male _' inglese.

ghe gal gle gno ca ce che ci sco pe Par por sco il
l la lia lo na ne no non

7. Break the flow: Draw a line between words

a. Parlobenel'ingleseel'italiano.

b. Sonotedescaeparlobeneilfrancese.

c. Sonocineseeparlobenelospagnolo.

d. Didovesei?Sonoscozzeseehocinqueanni.

e. Qualilingueparli?Parlomoltobenel'irlandese.

f. Non parlobenelospagnoloperòparloilcinese.

g. MichiamoCarloeparlomoltomaleilgallese.

8. Spot the Intruder

Identify the word in each sentence the speaker is NOT saying

a. Parlo bene l'inglese italiano però non sono inglese.

b. Sono australiana australiano e non parlo bene il cinese.

c. Parlo bene il tedesco, però sono anche italiano.

d. Parli bene lo spagnolo? Sí, parlo bene anche il lo portoghese.

e. Non parlo bene il gallese, e però parlo bene l'irlandese.

f. Sono portoghese e parlo bene portoghese l'italiano.

g. Non parlo bene il lo cinese

h. Sono americano americana e parlo bene lo spagnolo.

9. Catch it, Swap it

Listen, spot the difference between what you hear and the written text and edit each sentence accordingly

e.g. Sono <u>francese</u>

a. Sono italiana e parlo bene l'italiano e l'inglese.

b. Sono irlandese e parlo male lo spagnolo.

c. Sono americana e parlo bene lo spagnolo.

d. Sono americana e parlo male l'italiano.

e. Sono scozzese e parlo bene il tedesco.

f. Sono irlandese però non parlo bene il cinese.

g. Sono australiano e parlo bene il portoghese

inglese

10. Sentence bingo

Write 4 of the sentences into the grid. You will hear sentences in Italian in a RANDOM ORDER. Tick all 4 of your sentences to win bingo.

1. Parlo bene il francese.
2. Sono italiana.
3. Parlo bene il cinese.
4. Parlo bene il tedesco.
5. Sono inglese.
6. Non parlo bene l'inglese.
7. Sono portoghese.
8. Sono irlandese.
9. Parlo bene il gallese.
10. Non parlo bene il tedesco.

THE LANGUAGE GYM

11. Listening Slalom

Listen in Italian and pick the equivalent English words from each column.

e.g. Sono cinese e parlo bene cinese.

Colour in the boxes for each sentence in a different colour.

e.g.	*I am*	I am	but I do not speak	I speak Spanish.
a.	My name is Stefano	*Chinese and*	badly	German well.
b.	Hello	English	*I speak well*	French.
c.	I am	I speak Spanish	Italian and	*Chinese.*
d.	I speak	Spanish	but I am	Portuguese.
e.	You don't speak	Chinese well	and I also speak	English.
f.	I am not	Irish	I am from Argentina and I speak	but you speak Italian well.

Unit 7. Where I am from & languages I speak: READING

1. Sylla-Bees

Read and put the syllables in the cells in the correct order

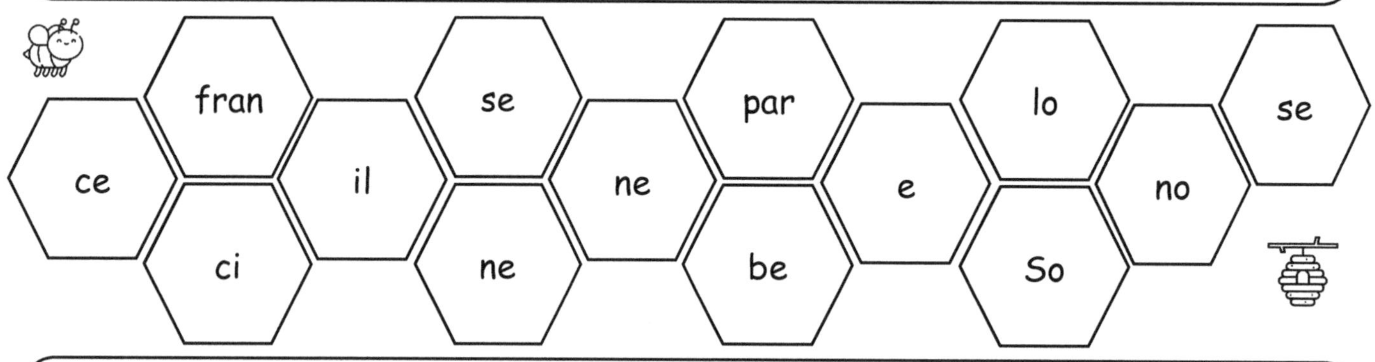

a. *I am French and I speak Chinese well.*

S_______ f__________ e p_______ b_______ i__ c__________.

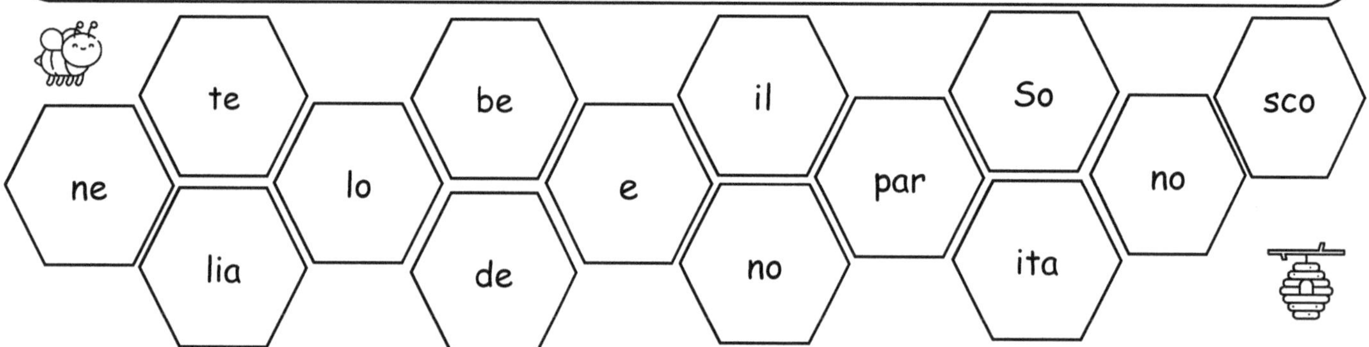

b. *I am Italian (m), and I speak German well.*

S______ i__________ e p______ b______ i__ t__________.

c. *I speak English badly.*

P___________ m_________ l'i___________.

THE LANGUAGE GYM

2. True or False

A. Read the paragraphs below and then answer True or False

Ciao, mi chiamo **Dario**. Ho tredici anni e ho una cagnolina che si chiama Lilla. Ha un anno ed è molto brava. Sono spagnolo e parlo bene l'inglese e il francese. Parlo anche bene il portoghese, però non parlo bene il tedesco. Mi piace molto lo spagnolo.

Ciao, mi chiamo **Simona**. Ho dodici anni e non ho animali. Sono italiana e parlo bene l'italiano e l'inglese. Parlo anche bene il francese, però parlo male il cinese. Mi piace molto parlare lo spagnolo, però non mi piace per niente parlare il cinese.

	True	False
a. **Dario** is 13 years old.		
b. He has a little cat.		
c. He speaks French well.		
d. He speaks English and French.		
e. He doesn't speak German.		
f. He doesn't like Spanish.		
g. **Simona** is French.		
h. She speaks Italian and English.		
i. She doesn't speak Chinese.		
j. She doesn't like speaking in Spanish.		

B. Find in the texts above the Italian for:

a. It is one year old.

b. It is very good.

c. I do not have pets.

d. I really like...

e. I like to speak...

f. I don't like it at all.

THE LANGUAGE GYM

3. Tick or Cross

A. Read the texts. Tick the box if you find the words in the text, cross it if you do not find them.

- Ciao, mi chiamo **Patrizia.**

Ho nove anni. Il mio compleanno è il quindici ottobre. Sono australiana e parlo bene l'inglese e l'italiano. Parlo anche bene il portoghese, però non parlo cinese. Mi piace molto il tedesco.

- Ciao, mi chiamo **Paolo.**

Ho otto anni. Sono scozzese e parlo bene l'inglese e il francese. Parlo anche bene l'irlandese, però non parlo bene l'italiano. Non mi piace per niente lo spagnolo.

	✓	✗
a. Ho otto anni.		
b. Sono francese.		
c. Il quindici ottobre.		
d. Parlo spagnolo.		
e. Non parlo cinese.		
f. Non mi piace.		

g. I am 6 years old.		
h. I am Spanish.		
i. I speak English.		
j. I speak Italian.		
k. I don't speak.		
l. I don't like at all.		

B. Find the Italian in the texts above

a. The 15th of October. _______________________________

b. I do not speak Chinese. _______________________________

c. I speak English well. _______________________________

d. I really like German. _______________________________

e. I do not like Spanish at all. _______________________________

4. Language Detective

- Mi chiamo **Riccardo.** <u>Ho cinque anni.</u> Il mio compleanno è il nove novembre. Sono americano e parlo bene il francese e il tedesco. Parlo anche bene il portoghese, però non parlo lo spagnolo. Non mi piace l'irlandese.

- Mi chiamo **Martina.** Ho tredici anni. Il mio compleanno è il dodici marzo. Ho un cavallo marrone che si chiama Artex. Sono irlandese e parlo molto bene l'irlandese e lo spagnolo. Parlo anche bene il cinese. Mi piace lo spagnolo.

- Ciao, mi chiamo **Carmela.** Ho undici anni. Il mio compleanno è il venti giugno. Sono spagnola e mi piace parlare l'inglese. Parlo molto bene lo spagnolo e il tedesco. Parlo bene anche il cinese, però parlo malissimo il francese.

A. Find someone who...

a. ...is 13 years old.

b. ...has a brown horse.

c. ...likes English.

d. ...speaks Chinese well (2).

e. ...speaks French very badly.

f. ...speaks German very well (2).

g. ...doesn't speak French.

B. Put a cross in the box and underline the corresponding Italian translation. One is odd.

I am five years old.	I like speaking English.	But I don't speak Spanish.
I also speak Portuguese well.	The 12th of March.	I also speak Chinese well.
I am American.	I really like Spanish.	I don't like Spanish.
I don't like Irish.	The 20th of June.	I am Spanish.

Unit 7. Where I am from & languages I speak: WRITING

---

1. Spelling

a. S __ __ o __ __ __ __ __ __ __ __ o   *I am German*

b. S __ __ __ m __ __ __ t __ b __ __ __ __   *I am very well*

c. N __ n s __ __ __ o p __ __ t __ __ h __ __ __ e   *I am not Portuguese*

d. __ ar __ __ __ __ ene __' __ __ __ __ l __ __ e   *I speak English well*

e. __ ar __ __ __ m __ __ e l'i __ __ __ __ __ se   *I speak English badly*

f. S __ __ o s __ __ __ __ n __ __ a   *I am Spanish*

g. P __ __ l __ be __ e i __ c __ __ __ __ __ __ __   *I speak Chinese well*

h. M __ c __ __ __ am__ M __ __ __ ia. __ t__?   *My name is Maria. And you?*

---

2. Anagrams: unscramble the Italian

a. arloP eneb ol lospagno   *I speak well Spanish.*

b. onN onos seglein   *I am not English.*

c. Nno noso pogheserto   *I am not Portuguese.*

d. iM cepia li leqalse.   *I like Welsh.*

e. noN rlopa li scodete.   *I don't speak German.*

3. Gapped Translation

a. Parlo bene il tedesco e il francese, però non parlo l'inglese.

I speak __________ and __________ well, but I don't speak __________ .

b. Sono tedesca e parlo molto bene l'irlandese.

I am __________ and I speak Irish __________ __________ .

c. Sono inglese, però parlo anche il francese.

I am __________ , but I __________ speak __________ .

d. Quali lingue parli? Parlo portoghese.

What __________ do you __________ ? I speak __________ .

e. Di dove sei? Sono americana però parlo male l'inglese.

__________ are you __________ ? I am American __________ I speak English __________ .

4. Split Sentences

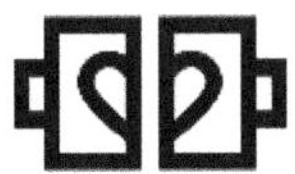

a. Parlo molto	**1.** parli?
b. Parlo male	**2.** portoghese.
c. Parlo male il	**3.** inglese.
d. Sono	**4.** bene l'inglese.
e. Non	**5.** il tedesco.
f. Che lingue	**6.** parlo bene il cinese.
g. Di dove	**7.** sei?

a	b	c	d	e	f	g

5. Rock Climbing

Starting from the bottom, pick one chunk from each row to translate the sentences below.

l'irlandese.	il francese.	il tedesco.	l'inglese.	lo spagnolo.
Parlo molto male	parlo bene	parlo molto bene	parlo male	non parlo bene
Sono inglese però	e	Mi chiamo Pietro e	Sono francese e	e non
ti chiami?	francese	il cinese	parli?	sei?
Sono	Parlo bene	Quali lingue	Di dove	Come
a.	**b.**	**c.**	**d.**	**e.**

a. *I am French and I don't speak German well.*

____

b. *I speak Chinese well, and I don't speak French badly.*

____

c. *What languages do you speak? I am French and I speak English very well.*

____

d. *Where are you from? I am English but I speak Spanish very badly.*

____

e. *What is your name? My name is Pietro and I speak Irish well.*

____

6. Mosaic Translation
Use the words in the grid to help you translate the sentences below.

a.	Sono	parli?	Sono americano	e parlo molto male	il cinese.
b.	Di dove	italiana	però	e parlo bene	l'inglese.
c.	Mi chiamo	sei?	Sono americana	male	il tedesco.
d.	Quali lingue	l'inglese	Parlo	mi piace anche	il francese.
e.	Parlo molto bene	Mario.	e parlo	bene	lo spagnolo.

a. *I am Italian and I speak French well.*

____

b. *Where are you from? I am American (f) and I speak Chinese well.*

____

c. *My name is Mario. I am American and I speak English very badly.*

____

d. *What languages do you speak? I speak German badly.*

____

e. *I speak English very well, but I also like Spanish.*

____

7. Fill in the Gaps

a. Ciao, mi chiamo Roberta. Ho ___________ anni. Il mio compleanno è ____ venti giugno. Sono ___________ e ___________ il tedesco e il ___________. Parlo ___________ bene l'inglese.

anche	italiana	otto	il	francese	parlo

b. Ciao, mi chiamo Paolo. Ho un cane _________. Sono francese e parlo molto _______ il tedesco e lo spagnolo. Parlo bene __________ il francese. Mi piace molto il ______________.

portoghese	nero	bene	anche

8. Tangled Translation

a. Write the Italian words in English to complete the translation

Hello, **mi chiamo** Michele. **Ho** seven years old. My birthday **è il tredici** of March. I am **francese.** I speak French and English **molto bene.** Also **parlo bene** Italian, **però** I don't speak **il tedesco.** I like **il cinese.**

b. Write the English words in Italian to complete the translation

Buongiorno, **my name is** Lorena. **I am** dodici anni. Il mio compleanno **is on the 4th** aprile. Ho **a dog** nero **who is called** Colli. Sono **German. I speak** molto bene l'inglese **and** parlo **also French,** però **I don't speak** italiano. **I like** il tedesco.

9. Sentence Puzzle
Put the words in each sentence in the correct order

a. molto Parlo l'inglese francese il l' e bene.

I speak English and French very well.

b. Quali spagnolo Parlo lingue parli? lo male

What language do you speak? I speak Spanish badly.

c. Di sei? australiana Sono dove parlo bene e tedesco il

Where are you from? I am Australian and I speak German well.

d. Inglese, Parlo però parlo non tedesco il bene.

I speak English but, I don't speak German well.

10. Guided Translation

a. C______, m__ c________ M________. S_____ a____________.

Hi, my name is Marta. I am Australian.

b. S______ s__________. P_________ m____ b________ l'i_________.

I am Spanish (f). I speak Italian very well.

c. P_____ m_____ b___ i_ f______ e p_______m _____ l'i________.

I speak French very well and I speak Irish badly.

d. P______ b_______ i_ t_________, p_____ n___ p______ i_ c______.

I speak German well, but I don't speak Chinese.

e. Q____ l______ p_______? P_______ m____ b____ i_ p__________.

What languages do you speak? I speak Portuguese well.

11. Pyramid Translation
Starting from the top, translate each chunk in Italian. Write the sentences in the box below.

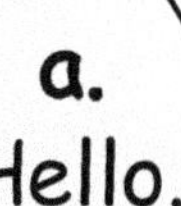

a.	
b.	
c.	
d.	
e.	

THE LANGUAGE GYM

12. Staircase Translation

Starting from the top, translate each chunk into Italian.
Write the sentences in the grid below.

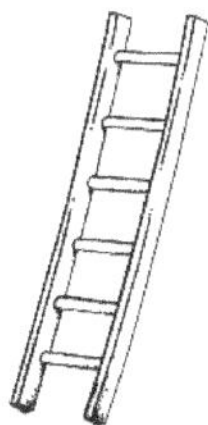

a.	I am	Irish.				
b.	I speak	English	well.			
c.	I do not speak	German well,	but I speak	Italian.		
d.	I speak	Chinese	very well,	but I do not speak	Spanish.	
e.	I am	Scottish.	I speak	Portuguese well,	but I don't speak	Irish.

Answers / Risposte

a.	
b.	
c.	
d.	
e.	

🏆 Challenge / Sfida

Can you create 2 more sentences using the words in the staircase grid above?

☆	
☆	

THE LANGUAGE GYM

UNIT 8
CHE TEMPO FA?

In this unit you will learn how to:

- ✓ Understand and use weather expressions
- ✓ Use time frames and seasons
- ✓ Use *fa/ c'è*
- ✓ Find a place on the map

You will revisit:
- ★ Countries, languages and nationalities
- ★ Names of Italian locations

Che tempo fa oggi?

Oggi c'è il sole

Unit 8. THE WEATHER
I can describe what the weather is like.

> **Che tempo fa?** *What is the weather like?*

In inverno *In winter*	**fa bel tempo** *it is good weather*		a Bari
			a Firenze
In autunno *In autumn*	**fa brutto tempo** *it is bad weather*		a Milano
In primavera *In spring*	**fa caldo** *it is hot*		a Napoli
	fa freddo *it is cold*		a Palermo
In estate *In summer*	**c'è nebbia** *it is foggy*		a Pisa
Di solito *Usually*	**c'è il sole** *it is sunny*		a Roma
			a Sorrento
Oggi *Today*	**c'è un temporale** *it is stormy*		a Venezia
Normalmente *Normally*	**c'è vento** *it is windy*		in Australia
Questa settimana *This week*	**è nuvoloso** *it is cloudy*		in Inghilterra
			in Irlanda
	nevica *it snows*		in Italia
	piove *it rains*		

Unit 8. What the weather is like: LISTENING

1. Listen and tick the word you hear

	1	2	3
a.	Fa bel tempo	Fa freddo	Fa caldo
b.	C'è un temporale	C'è vento	C'è nebbia
c.	Nevica	C'è nebbia	È nuvoloso
d.	Fa brutto tempo	Fa bel tempo	Che tempo fa?
e.	C'è il sole	C'è un temporale	C'è vento
f.	Fa brutto tempo	Fa bel tempo	È nuvoloso
g.	C'è il sole	C'è nebbia	C'è vento

2. Faulty Echo

e.g. *Oggi c'è il sole.*

a. In inverno fa freddo.

b. Normalmente piove.

c. In estate fa caldo.

d. Oggi c'è un temporale.

e. Di solito fa bel tempo.

f. Che tempo fa?

g. Questa settimana c'è nebbia.

3. Listen and Match

a. Today

b. Normally

c. In summer

d. In autumn

e. In winter

f. This week

g. In spring

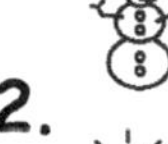

1.

2.

3.

4.

5.

6.

7.

a	b	c	d	e	f	g

4. Listen and complete with the missing letters

a. __ freddo.

b. __ vento.

c. Oggi __ nuvoloso.

d. __ brutto tempo.

e. __ caldo.

f. __ il sole.

g. In inverno __ nebbia.

h. __ nuvoloso.

i. __ un temporale.

5. Listen and complete with the missing syllable

a. In primavera pi__ __ __.

b. Oggi fa b__ __ tempo.

c. In autunno fa fre__ __ __.

d. In inverno __ __ __ica.

e. Di sol__ __ __ c'è il sole.

f. In __ __ __ate fa caldo.

g. Normalmente __ __ nebbia.

ddo est el nev ove ito c'è

6. Can you help the penguin to break the flow? Draw a line between words

a. Chetempofa?Oggic'èilsole.

b. InestatefacaldoaSorrento.

c. InautunnofabeltempoaRoma.

d. IninvernofafreddoaVenezia.

e. Disolitoènuvolosoa Milano.

f. Oggic'èventoepioveaFirenze.

g. Normalmentec'èilsoleaBari.

h. QuestasettimanapioveinAustralia.

7. Complete with the missing syllables in the box below

a. In Australia fa bel _ _ _ po.

b. In Italia c'è _ _ sole.

c. In Inghilterra _ _ _ ve.

d. A Palermo c'è _ _ _to .

e. A Bari è _ _ voloso.

f. A Venezia in in _ _ _ no nevica.

g. A Pisa in primave _ _ piove.

h. A Firenze og _ _ fa brutto tempo.

i. Questa set _ _ mana c'è nebbia.

j. In autunno fa _ _ _ _ do.

tem ven il nu fred pio ver ra gi ti

8. Fill in the grid with the correct information in English

	When	Weather
a.		
b.		
c.		
d.		
e.		
f.		

9. Spot the Intruder

Identify the word in each sentence the speaker is NOT saying

e.g. Oggi c'è <u>fa</u> il sole

a. Che tempo no fa a Milano?

b. A Firenze c'è piove questa settimana.

c. In Australia fa freddo caldo in estate.

d. Di solito c'è a il sole a Napoli.

e. A Venezia fa c'è nebbia.

f. In autunno fa il freddo.

114

10. Listening Slalom

Listen in Italian and pick the 3 equivalent English parts from each column.

e.g. Oggi fa caldo a Sorrento.

You could colour each sentence in a different colour. Then, read the sentence out loud.

e.g.	*Today*	it is windy	in England.
a.	Normally	*it is hot*	in Venice.
b.	In spring	it is bad weather	*in Sorrento.*
c.	In autumn	it is cold	in Australia.
d.	Today	it is good weather	in Bari.
e.	Usually	it rains	in Palermo.
f.	This week	it snows	in Florence.
g.	Today	it is sunny	in Pisa.

Unit 8. What the weather is like: READING

1. Sylla-Bees

Read and put the syllables in the cells in the correct order

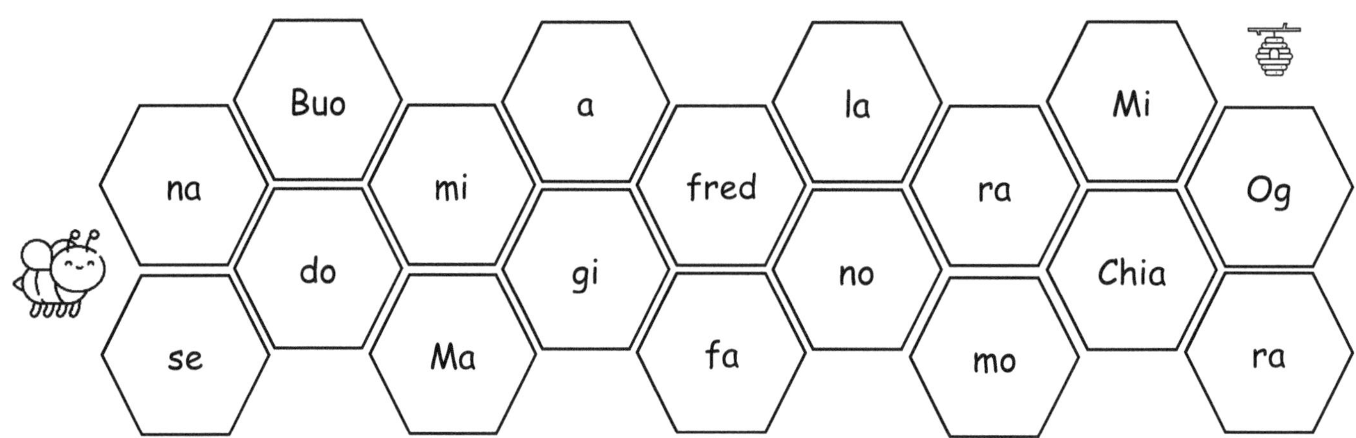

a. Good evening, my name is Mara. Today in Milan it is cold.

B_______ s________, m__ c______________ M__________.
O______ a M________ f____ f_______.

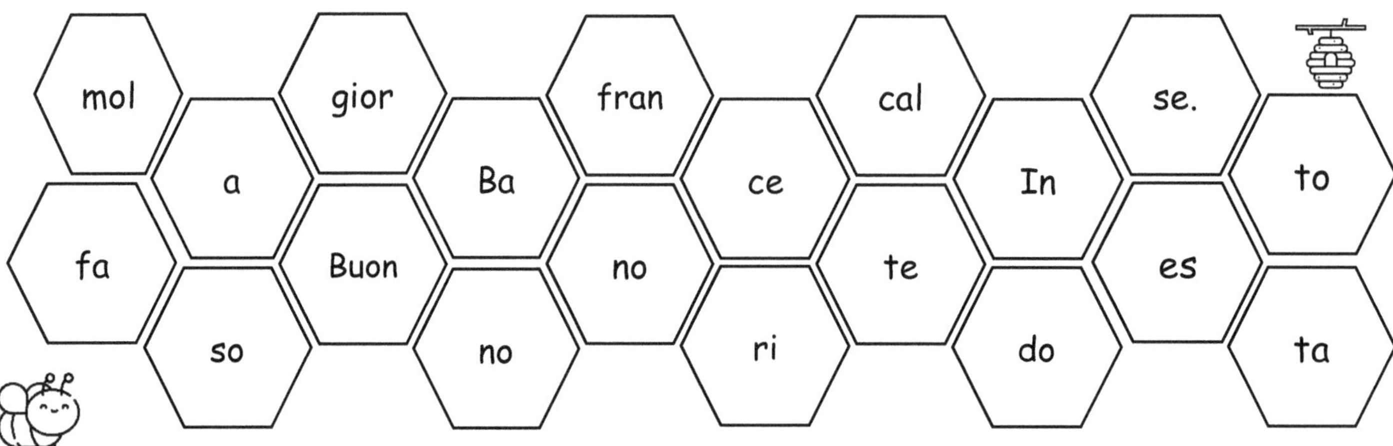

b. Good morning, I am French. In summer in Bari it is very hot. 

B__________, s_______ f__________. I__ e__________
a B__________ f______ m________ c________.

THE LANGUAGE GYM

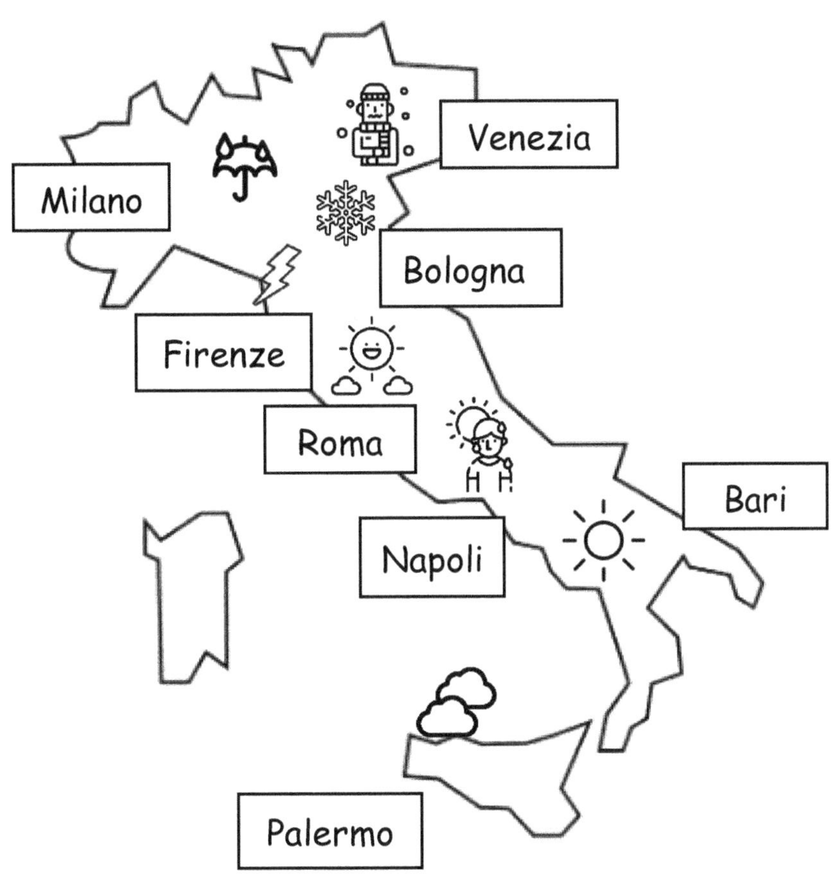

a. Oggi a Roma fa freddo.

b. Normalmente a Venezia c'è vento.

c. A Palermo è nuvoloso.

d. Di solito a Firenze fa bel tempo.

e. Questa settimana a Milano piove.

f. Normalmente a Napoli c'è un temporale.

g. Oggi a Bologna nevica.

h. In estate a Bari c'è il sole.

	True	False
a.		
b.		
c.		
d.		
e.		
f.		
g.		
h.		

3. Read, Match, Find and Colour

A. Match these sentences to the pictures above

a. Questa settimana nevica a Milano.
b. Normalmente c'è il sole a Bari.
c. C'è un temporale a Bologna.
d. In inverno piove a Roma.
e. In autunno fa vento a Sorrento.
f. In primavera fa bel tempo.
g. Normalmente è nuvoloso in Inghilterra.
h. In estate fa caldo a Palermo.
i. Oggi fa brutto tempo a Pisa.
j. Questa settimana fa freddo a Firenze.

B. Using the sentences in task A find the Italian for:

a. It is hot.
b. It is cloudy.
c. In winter.
d. It is good weather.
e. This week.
f. It is cold.
g. It rains.
h. Today.
i. It is sunny.
j. It is windy.

4. True of False?
A. Read the paragraphs below and then answer True or False

	True	False
a. **Davide** is fourteen years old.		
b. He speaks French very well.		
c. He is from Germany.		
d. It is normally warm in France.		
e. It is normally cold in France.		
f. It is raining in France today.		
g. **Paola** is French.		
h. In Germany there is never bad weather.		
i. She speaks German very well.		
j. It is warm in Germany today.		

B. Find in the texts above the Italian for:

a. But today.

b. It is normally warm.

c. In Germany it is usually bad weather.

d. But there is bad weather today.

5. Language Detective

- Il mio nome è **Pietro**. Il mio compleanno è il dodici dicembre. Sono scozzese e parlo bene l'inglese e il francese, ma non parlo cinese. A Edimburgo di solito in inverno ci sono i temporali, ma oggi fa caldo e non piove.

- Mi chiamo **Carmela**. Il mio compleanno è l'undici dicembre. Sono spagnola e parlo benissimo lo spagnolo. Parlo anche l'italiano. In estate di solito fa bel tempo a Madrid, ma oggi è nuvoloso e c'è un po' di vento.

- Ciao, il mio nome è **Daniele**. Ho dodici anni. Il mio compleanno è il tredici dicembre. Vivo in Italia. A Roma in primavera normalmente fa bel tempo, ma oggi piove e fa freddo. Non mi piace quando fa freddo.

A. Read & answer the questions

a. Who lives in Italy?

b. Who doesn't speak Chinese?

c. Where isn't it raining today?

d. Where is it raining today?

e. Where is there usually good weather in summer?

f. Who does speak Italian?

g. Where is it cloudy today?

h. Where is normally good weather in spring?

B. Put a cross in the box and underline the corresponding Italian translation. Two are odd.

~~I am from Ireland.~~	I speak English and French.	I have a white and grey cat.
I am English.	I don't like when it is cold.	I also speak Italian.
But it rains today.	My birthday is on the 11th of December.	It is a bit windy.
But it is cloudy today.	My birthday is on the 12th of December.	It is warm today.

Unit 8. What the weather is like: WRITING

1. Spelling

a. I __ p __ __ __ a __ __ __ __.   *In spring.*

b. I__ e __ __ a __ e c'__ i __ so __ __.   *In summer it's sunny.*

c. O __ __ __ f__ c __ __ __ o.   *It's warm today.*

d. I __ a __ __ __ __ n __.   *In autumn.*

e. I __ i __ __ __ __ __ n __ n __ __ __ __ __ a.   *In winter it snows.*

f. I __ a __ __ __ n __ o p __ __ __ e.   *In autumn it rains.*

g. I __ e __ __ __ __ __ e f __ c __ l __ __.   *In summer it is warm.*

2. Gapped Translation

a. Sono australiana e oggi fa bel tempo.

I _____ Australian and there is _________ weather __________.

b. In autunno c'è vento a Firenze.

In ______________ it is _________ in __________.

c. Sono inglese e normalmente fa brutto tempo in Inghilterra.

I am English and ___________ there is ______ weather in __________.

d. Sono scozzese e di solito non fa bel tempo.

I am _____________ and __________ there is not _________ weather.

e. Oggi è nuvoloso e c'è vento ma non c'è un temporale.

_________ it is ___________ and ________, but there is no storm.

f. Questa settimana fa caldo a Bari però piove e fa freddo a Venezia.

This _______ it's _______ in Bari but _______ and it's _______ in Venice.

3. Fill in the gaps

a. Ciao mi chiamo Carlo. Ho ______________ anni. Sono ______________. A Londra, di ___________ fa __________ e _________, _________ oggi fa caldo.

| ma | piove | quattordici | inglese | solito | freddo |

b. Ciao ______ chiamo Giulia. Sono italiana e _________ dieci anni. ____ Italia in __________ fa _________ tempo, ma oggi è ___________ e piove.

| ho | mi | estate | bel | nuvoloso | In |

4. Sentence Puzzle
Put the words in the correct order

a. Italia fa tempo bel In

It is good weather in Italy.

b. Inghilterra In fa tempo brutto piove e

In England it is bad weather and it rains.

c. Che fa Italia? tempo in Normalmente il c'è sole

What is the weather like in Italy? Normally it is sunny.

d. Oggi e vento, c'è piove c'è non temporale un ma

Today it rains and it is windy, but there is no storm.

e. Di Milano nevica freddo in e a inverno solito fa

Usually in winter it is cold and snows in Milan.

No Snakes No Ladders

PARTENZA	1 Sono inglese	2 Sono spagnola	3 Parlo spagnolo	4 Sono scozzese	5 Non parlo	6 Non parlo bene il gallese	7 Fa caldo
15 Però non parlo	14 Di dove sei?	13 Sono cinese	12 Oggi c'è nebbia	11 Fa freddo	10 Parlo bene il francese	9 In estate	8 Che tempo fa?
16 C'è vento	17 Fa bel tempo	18 In inverno	19 In primavera	20 Quali lingue parli?	21 Parlo bene l'inglese	22 Sono tedesco	23 Parlo male l'italiano
ARRIVO	30 Nevica a Firenze	29 Parlo molto bene il tedesco	28 C'è il sole a Roma	27 È nuvoloso a Milano	26 Piove a Bari	25 Questa settimana	24 Oggi c'è un temporale

No Snakes No Ladders

PARTENZA 	1 I am English	2 I am Spanish (f)	3 I speak Spanish	4 I am Scottish	5 I don't speak	6 I don't speak Welsh well	7 It is hot
15 But I don't speak	14 Where are you from?	13 I am Chinese	12 Today it is foggy	11 It is cold	10 I speak French well	9 In summer	8 What is the weather like?
16 It is windy	17 It is good weather	18 In winter	19 In spring	20 What languages do you speak?	21 I speak English well	22 I am German (m)	23 I speak Italian badly
ARRIVO	30 It snows in Florence	29 I speak German very well	28 It is sunny in Rome	27 It is cloudy in Milan	26 It rains in Bari	25 This week	24 It is stormy today

UNIT 9
LA MIA CITTÁ

In this unit you will learn how to say in Italian:

- ✓ Where you live
- ✓ Say if you like/ dislike your town and why
- ✓ Use *vivo/vivi*

You will revisit:

- ★ How to use *amo/mi piace/non mi piace/odio*
- ★ Masculine/ feminine adjectival agreement
- ★ Word order noun + adjective

Vivo a Milano

Adoro la mia città perché è bella

Dove vivi? *Where do you live?*
Ti piace la tua città? *Do you like your city?*

| Vivo a
I live in | Edimburgo
Edinburgh

Milano

Palermo

Leeds

Londra
London

Lugano

Madrid

New York
New York

Roma
Rome

Sidney

Torino | amo
I love

mi piace
I like

non mi piace
I don't like

odio
I hate | il mio paese
my town

la mia città
my city | perché è
because it is

perché non è
because it is not | bello *pretty*
brutto *ugly*
piccolo *small*
rumoroso *noisy*
tranquillo *quiet*
turistico *touristic*

grande *big*
vivace *lively*

bella
brutta
piccola
rumorosa
tranquilla
turistica |

THE LANGUAGE GYM

1. Listen and tick the word you hear

	1	2	3
a.	Londra	vivo	paese
b.	Mi piace	città	bello
c.	bella	paese	odio
d.	vivace	rumorosa	grande
e.	amo	tranquillo	vivo

2. Faulty Echo

e.g. *Vivo a Bar̲cellona.*

a. Mi piace il mio paese.

b. Amo la mia città.

c. Non mi piace la mia città.

d. Vivo a Londra.

e. Il mio paese è piccolo.

f. La mia città è brutta.

g. Perché è rumorosa.

h. Perché è tranquillo.

3. Listen and complete with the missing letters

a. Vivo __ New York.

b. La mia ci__tà è bell__.

c. Il mio pa__se è pic__olo.

d. Viv__ a Edi__burgo.

e. La m__a città è tranquill__.

f. Il mio paese è bell__.

g. Il mio paes__ è tranquill__.

h. M__ piace la mi__ città.

i. Non mi p__ace il mio pa__se.

j. La mia citt__ è picco__a.

THE LANGUAGE GYM

4. Narrow Listening. Gap-fill

a. Ciao, mi chiamo Killian e ho undici __________. Sono __________________,

però vivo ______ Inghilterra. Parlo ________ l'inglese e parlo molto

__________ l'irlandese e ________________. Mi piace il mio

______________ perché è tranquillo e ________________.

spagnolo	in	bene	irlandese	paese	anni	bene	bello

b. Ciao, mi chiamo Rosa e ho __________ anni. Sono ______, però ________

in Germania. Parlo __________, spagnolo e __________. Amo la mia

__________ perché ____ grande, però __________.

vivo	tedesco	undici	città	rumorosa	è	spagnola	francese

5. Fill in the grid with the correct information in English

		Opinion	Reason (Adjective)
a.	Ernesto		
b.	Antonio		
c.	Stefano		
d.	Carlotta		
e.	Michele		
f.	Gianfranco		

6. Complete with the missing letters in the box below

a. Vivo _ Madrid.

b. _ _ piace il mio paese.

c. Mi piace la _ _ _ città.

d. O _ _ _ la mia città.

e. A _ _ il mio paese.

f. _ _ _ mi piace il mio paese.

g. La mia città _ brutta.

h. Il mio _ _ _ se è brutto.

i. _ _ piace il tuo paese?

j. Il mio paese è _ _ moroso.

mo	Ti	pae	ru	a	Mi	è	mia	dio	Non	

7. Spot the Intruder

Identify the word in each sentence the speaker is NOT saying

a. Vivo a Londra. Mi piace la mia città perché non è bella.

b. Vivo a Trani. Non mi piace il mio ma paese perché è piccolo.

c. Vivo a Roma e odio la mia città perché è molto rumorosa.

d. Amo la mia città perché è grande, bella e vivace.

e. Non mi piace la mia città perché è tranquilla.

f. Dove vivi? Vivo a in New York. Mi piace perché è grande.

g. Mi piace il mio paese perché dove è turistico.

h. Mi non mi piace Leeds perché è brutta.

8. Catch it, Swap it.

Listen, spot the difference between what you hear and the written text and edit each sentence accordingly

e.g. Non mi piace la mia città perché non è <u>bella</u>.

	tranquilla

    a. Non mi piace il mio paese perché è piccolo.

    b. Odio la mia città perché è molto grande.

    c. Amo la mia città perché è tranquilla.

    d. Non mi piace la mia città perché è vivace.

    e. Mi piace il mio paese perché è tranquillo.

    f. Amo New York perché è vivace.

    g. Non mi piace la mia città perché è brutta.

9. Sentence bingo

Write 4 of the sentences into the grid. You will hear sentences in Italian in a RANDOM ORDER. Tick all 4 of your sentences to win!

1. Non mi piace il mio paese perché è piccolo.

2. Non mi piace il mio paese perché è brutto.

3. Mi piace la mia città perché è molto bella.

4. Amo la mia città perché è tranquilla.

5. Odio la mia città perché è molto grande.

6. Mi piace il mio paese perché è tranquillo.

7. Non mi piace la mia città perché è orribile.

8. Mi piace la mia città perché è grande.

9. Odio la mia città perché è brutta.

10. Amo New York perché è vivace.

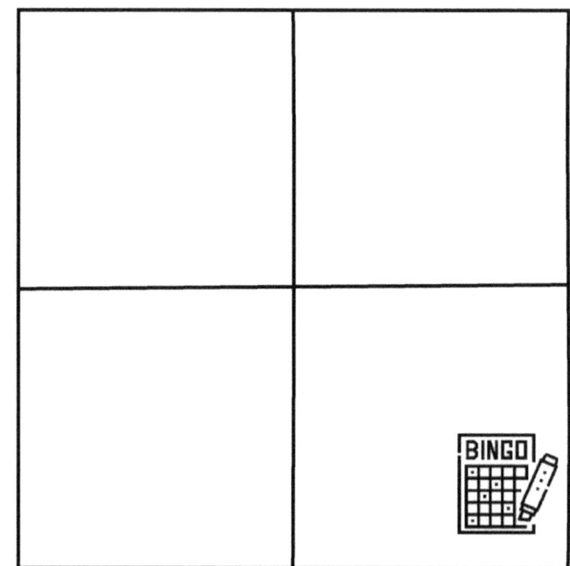

10. Listening Slalom

Listen in Italian and pick the equivalent English words from each column.

e.g. Mi chiamo Gianni, vivo in Madrid. Amo la mia città.

Colour in the boxes for each sentence in a different colour.

e.g.	*My name is Gianni*	because it is pretty	lively and touristic.
a.	I live in New York	*I live in Madrid*	and quiet.
b.	I live in Fiesole	I love my city	*I love my city.*
c.	I don't like	It is big	because it is lively.
d.	I like my town	I like my town	and big.
e.	I hate my city	my town because	because it is touristic.
f.	I live in London	because it is ugly	it is small.

Unit 9: Where I live: READING

1. Read and put the syllables in the cells in the correct order

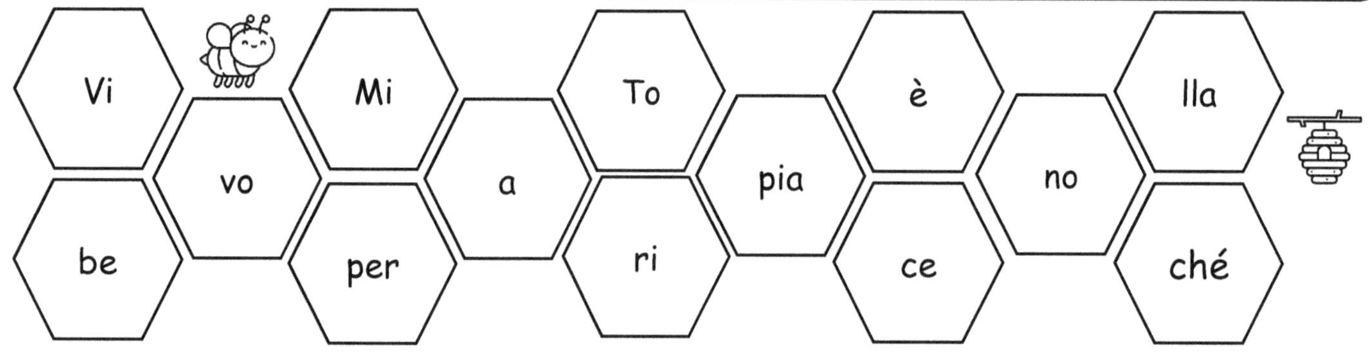

a. *I live in Torino. I like it because it is pretty.*

V_________ a__ T_________. M__ p_________ p_________ è
b_________.

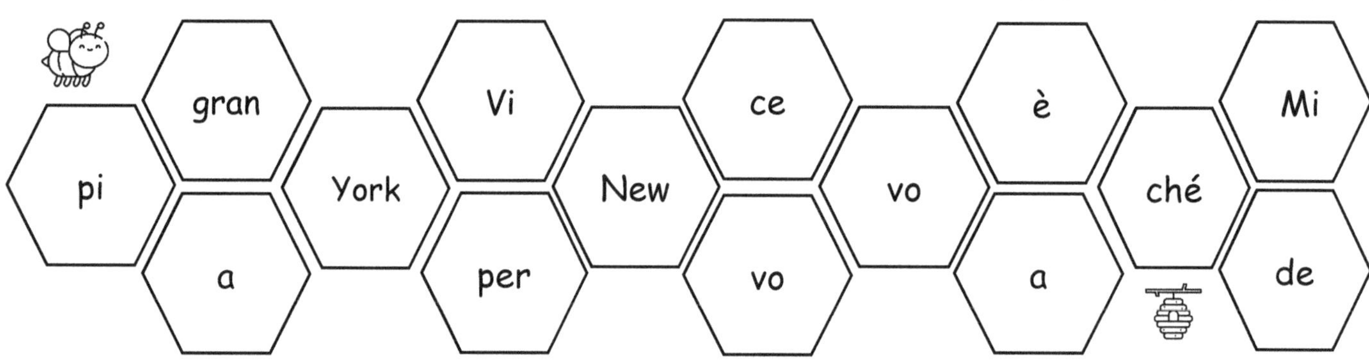

b. *I live in New York. I like it because it is big.*

V_________ a N_________ Y_________. M__ p_________
p_________ è g_________.

c. *My city is calm.*

L___ m____ c_________ è t_________.

THE LANGUAGE GYM

2. True or False
A. Read the paragraphs below and then answer True or False

	True	False
a. Luca is 15 years old.		
b. He speaks well English.		
c. He lives in Paris.		
d. It is normally cold in France.		
e. He likes his city.		
f. His city is big and lively.		
g. Beatrice is German.		
h. It is generally cold in Germany.		
i. She lives in Germany.		
j. She likes her town because it is calm.		

B. Find in the texts above the Italian for:

a. It is normally warm. **b.** It is small and pretty. **c.** I love.

d. It is usually cold. **e.** It is big and touristic. **f.** I live in Paris.

THE LANGUAGE GYM

3. Tick or Cross

A. Read the texts. Tick the box if you find the words in the text, cross it if you do not find them.

- Ciao, mi chiamo **Patrizia.**

Ho dieci anni. Sono spagnola e parlo molto bene lo spagnolo e il tedesco. Vivo a Barcellona. Oggi a Barcellona piove. Mi piace la mia città perché è vivace, però è molto rumorosa.

- Ciao, mi chiamo **Paolo.**

Ho sette anni. Sono italiana e parlo molto bene l'italiano, però non parlo il francese. Vivo a Roma. Qui normalmente c'è il sole. Odio la mia città perché è turistica e rumorosa. Preferisco una città tranquilla.

	✓	✗
a. Ho dieci anni.		
b. Sono francese.		
c. Parlo male		
d. Vivo a Parigi.		
e. Non mi piace.		
f. È vivace.		

g. I am 6 years old.		
h. I am Spanish.		
i. I hate my city.		
j. I speak French.		
k. Because it's sunny.		
l. Because it is noisy.		
m. A calm city.		

B. Find the Italian in the texts above

a. Today in Barcelona it is raining. ______________________________

b. I prefer a calm city. ______________________________

c. Here it is normally sunny. ______________________________

d. I hate my city because it is touristic. ______________________________

e. Because it is lively, but is very noisy. ______________________________

4. Language Detective

- Mi chiamo **Riccardo.** Il mio compleanno è il tre dicembre. Non ho animali. Sono <u>irlandese,</u> però vivo in Inghilterra, a Londra. Mi piace la mia città perché è vivace e turistica, però normalmente fa brutto tempo.

- Mi chiamo **Carlo.** Ho tredici anni. Ho un cane bianco e nero che si chiama Bobby. Sono spagnolo e vivo a Tossa de Mar. Amo il mio paese perché è tranquillo e bello. Di solito anche il tempo è bello.

- Ciao, mi chiamo **Daniela.** Ho undici anni. Ho un gatto bianco e grigio che si chiama Gigetto. Sono italiana, però vivo in America, a Detroit. Non mi piace la mia città perché è brutta e rumorosa. Oggi a Detroit piove.

A. Find someone who…

a. …is 11 years old.

b. …has a black and white dog.

c. …lives in a town.

d. …has a white and grey cat.

e. …lives in an ugly and noisy place.

f. …lives in a lively place.

g. …doesn't own a cat.

h. …lives in America

i. …lives in a calm place

B. Put a cross in the box and underline the corresponding Italian translation. One is odd.

~~I am from Ireland.~~	But I live in America.	I have a white and grey cat.
I don't have any pets.	I like my town.	I have a white and black dog.
Because it is calm and pretty.	I like my city.	It is raining in Detroit today.
Because it is ugly and noisy.	I don't like my city.	The weather is also usually good.

Unit 9: Where I live: WRITING

1. Spelling

a. V__ __ a __ __   *Lively*

b. R__ __ __ __ __ s __   *Noisy*

c. N__ __ __ __ __ p __ __ s __.   *In my town.*

d. L__ m__ __ c __ __ __ __   *My city*

e. P__ __ __ __ l __   *Small*

f. L__ m__ __ c __ __ __ __ __ è b__ __ tt __.   *My city is ugly.*

g. V __ __ __ __ __ L __ __ __ r __.   *I live in London.*

h. L __ m __ __ c __ __ __ à è b __ l __ __.   *My city is pretty.*

i. I __ __ i __ p __ __ __ __ è b __ __ l __.   *My town is pretty.*

2. Anagrams: unscramble the Italian

a. oviV ni teIlia a amoR   *I live in Italy, in Rome.*

b. iM cepia tolmo Lodran.   *I really like London.*

c. oidO li oim eseap   *I hate my town.*

d. ércheP è vaveci.   *Because it is lively.*

136

THE LANGUAGE GYM

3. Gapped Translation

a. Sono australiana, però vivo in Scozia.

I_________ Australian, but I __________ in Scotland.

b. Mi piace il mio paese perché molto bello e grande.

I like my __________ because it is _________ pretty and __________.

c. Vivo a Londra. Amo la mia città.

I____________ in London. I _____________ my _____________.

d. Ti piace il tuo paese? No, non mi piace il mio paese.

Do you like _______ town? No, I don't like _______ town.

e. Dove vivi? Vivo in un paese vivace, però piccolo.

Where do ______ _________? I live in a _________ but __________ town.

4. Split Sentences

a. Vivo in

b. Non parlo bene

c. Sono

d. Mi piace

e. perchè

f. Perchè è

g. Amo il mio

1. è bella.

2. paese.

3. la mia città.

4. spagnola.

5. turistico.

6. il francese

7. Inghilterra.

a	b	c	d	e	f	g

5. Rock Climbing

Starting from the bottom, pick one chunk from each row to translate the sentences below.

	a.	b.	c.	d.	e.	f.
	è brutto.	a Roma.	brutta.	è grande.	a Edimburgo.	piccola.
	Vivo	No, perché	però vivo	perché non è	perché	perché è
	la mia città	inglese	il tuo paese?	il mio paese	mia città	vivi?
	Sono	Non mi piace	Ti piace	Mi piace	Dove	Amo la

a. I am English but I live in Rome.

____

b. I don't like my city because it is ugly.

____

c. Do you like your town? No, because it is ugly.

____

d. I like my town because it is big.

____

e. Where do you live? I live in Edinburgh.

____

f. I love my city because it is not small.

____

6. Mosaic Translation
Use the words in the grid to help you translate the sentences below.

a.	La mia città	è bella	e bello.	amo	vivace.
b.	Dove	la tua città?	e piccola,	È anche	grande.
c.	Non mi piace	vivi?	Mi piace	però non è	turistica.
d.	Ti piace	Roma.	Vivo in	perchè è	rumoroso.
e.	Il mio paese	è tranquillo	perchè è	brutto e	Londra.
f.	Vivo a	il mio paese	Sí,	un paese	piccolo.

a. *My city is pretty and small, but it is touristic.*

____

b. *Where do you live? I live in a big town.*

____

c. *I don't like my town because it is ugly and noisy.*

____

d. *Do you like your city? Yes, I love London.*

____

e. *My town is calm and pretty. It is also small.*

____

f. *I live in Rome. I like it because it is lively.*

____

7. Fill in the gaps

a. Ciao, mi chiamo Simone. Ho __________ anni. Sono ___________, però vivo ____ Inghilterra. ___________ bene il tedesco. Mi piace il mio _____________ perché ____ tranquillo.

in	Parlo	dodici	è	paese	spagnolo

b. Ciao, mi chiamo Giulia. Sono italiana, però ________ a _________. Parlo molto _______ l'inglese e l'italiano. Parlo anche ____ spagnolo. Amo la mia _______ perché è tranquilla ___ bella.

città	e	vivo	bene	Glasgow	lo

8. Tangled Translation

a. Write the Italian words in English to complete the translation

Hello, **mi chiamo** Consuelo. **Sono** Spanish, **però** I live **in Germania**. I speak German **e spagnolo** well. In Germany, **normalmente**, it rains. I live **a Berlino e** I don't like it **perché è** very big and **rumorosa.**

b. Write the English words in Italian to complete the translation

Buongiorno, **my name is** Gianni. Ho **eleven** anni e **I don't have** animali. Vivo **a New York**. Amo la **my city** perché è **very big** e **pretty**. Mi piace **also because** è vivace e **it is not** brutta. A New York, **normally** fa bel **weather and** fa **warm.**

9. Sentence Puzzle

Put the words in the correct order

a. bella piace molto è Mi mia la città perché.

I like my city because it is very pretty.

b. Dove Vivo New York a piace non mi e vivi?

Where do you live? I live in New York and I don't like it.

c. Ti piace amo lo è perché piccolo tuo il paese?

Do you like your town? I love it because it is small.

d. Londra rumorosa è perché molto Odio turistica e anche.

I hate London because it is very noisy and also touristic.

10. Guided Translation

a. C______, m__ c_________ P_________. V______ a R_________.
Hi, my name is Patrizia. I live in Rome.

b. S________ s_________ p ______ v_______ i___ I____________.
I am Spanish (f) but I live in England.

c. V_____ i__ u__ p_______ b________. M__ p_______ p_______ è
t____________.
I live in a pretty town. I like it because it is calm.

d. L___ m__ c________ è v_________ e a__________ t____________.
My city is lively and also touristic.

e. D_______ v______? V________ a N_______ Y_______.

Where do you live? I live in New York.

11. Pyramid Translation

Starting from the top, translate each chunk in Italian. Write the sentences in the box below.

a.
Hello.

b. Hello, my name is Carlotta.

c. Hello, my name is Carlotta. I live in London.

d. Hello, my name is Carlotta. I live in London. I like my city because it is big and pretty.

e. Hello, my name is Carlotta. I live in London. I like my city because it is big and pretty, but it is not touristic.

a.

b.

c.

d.

e.

12. Staircase Translation

Starting from the top, translate each chunk into Italian.
Write the sentences in the grid below.

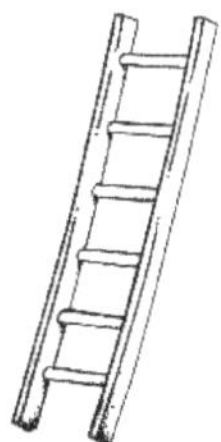

a.	I like	my city.				
b.	I don't like	my town because	it is touristic.			
c.	I love	my town beacuse	it is pretty	and lively.		
d.	I hate	my city because	it is big,	touristic	and also noisy.	
e.	I really like	my town because	it is pretty,	small	and also	quiet.

Answers / Risposte

a.

b.

c.

d.

e.

Challenge / Sfida

Can you create 2 more sentences using the words in the staircase grid above?

☆

☆

UNIT 10
NEL MIO PAESE

In this unit you will learn how to:

- Say what's in your town
- Practise singular and plural nouns

You will revisit:
- ★ How to use *c'è/non c'è*
- ★ *Un/una*
- ★ Saying where you live
- ★ Giving your opinion on your town

Nel mio quartiere c'è una piscina

Nel mio paese ci sono ristoranti

Unit 10. I can say what's in my town

Nel mio paese *In my town*	**c'è** *there is*	**un castello** *a castle* **un cinema** *a cinema* **un museo** *a museum* **un negozio** *a shop* **un parco** *a park* **un ristorante** *a restaurant* **uno stadio** *a stadium* **un supermercato** *a supermarket* **un teatro** *a theatre*	**ma non ci sono** *but there are not*	**castelli** *castles* **cinema** *cinemas* **musei** *museums* **negozi** *shops* **parchi** *parks* **ristoranti** *restaurants* **scuole** *schools* **stadi** *stadiums* **supermercati** *supermarkets*
Nella mia città *In my city* Nel mio quartiere *In my neighbour-hood*	**non c'è** *there is not*	**una biblioteca** *a library* **una cattedrale** *a cathedral* **una chiesa** *a church* **una farmacia** *a pharmacy* **una palestra** *a gym* **una panetteria** *a bakery* **una piazza** *a square* **una piscina** *a swimming pool* **una scuola** *a school* **una spiaggia** *a beach* **una stazione dei treni** *a train station*	**e ci sono anche** *and there are also*	**biblioteche** *libraries* **cattedrali** *cathedrals* **chiese** *churches* **farmacie** *pharmacies* **palestre** *gyms* **panetterie** *bakeries* **piazze** *squares* **piscine** *swimming pools* **scuole** *schools* **spiagge** *beaches* **stazioni dei treni** *train stations*

Unit 10. I can say what's in my town: LISTENING

1. Listen and tick the word you hear

	1	2	3
a.	piscina	piazza	stazione dei treni
b.	cinema	città	chiesa
c.	c'è	non c'è	anche
d.	negozio	teatro	teatri
e.	stadi	chiese	Nel mio paese

2. Faulty Echo

You will listen to each sentence twice. The first one is correct, and the second one has an incorrect sound. Underline the wrong word in each sentence.

e.g. Nel mio <u>paese</u> c'è un cinema.

a. Nella mia città c'è una chiesa.

b. Nel mio paese c'è una biblioteca.

c. Nella mia città ci sono ristoranti e parchi.

d. Nel mio paese non ci sono piscine.

e. Nel mio paese c'è una palestra e un castello.

f. Nella mia città c'è una piazza.

3. Listen and complete with the missing vowels

a. Il mio paes__

b. Una pi__zza

c. Una pisc__na

d. La mia c__ttà

e. Un cin__ma

f. Un m__seo

g. Una pal__stra

h. Una p__netteria

i. Una ch__esa

j. C'è una sp__aggia

a
e
i
o
u

4. Complete with the missing syllables in the box below

a. Un supermer _ _ to

b. Un tea _ _ _

c. Neg _ _ _

d. Sc _ _ le

e. Un par _ _

f. Una far _ _ cia

g. Una bi _ _ _ _ _ teca

h. Un caste _ _ _

i. Ris _ _ _ anti

j. La mia _ _ttà

| uo | ca | ma | ozi | co | blio | llo | ci | tor | tro | llo |

5. Fill in the grid with the information in English

	There is *(c'è)*	There is not *(non c'è)*
a.		
b.		
c.		
d.		

147

6. Spot the Intruder

Identify the words the speaker is NOT saying

e.g. *Nel mio quartiere c'è una piscina, <u>una chiesa</u> e una palestra.*

a. Nel mio paese ci sono ristoranti e un scuole.

b. Mi piace la città perché non c'è una piscina e una biblioteca.

c. Vivo a Londra. Nella mia città ci sono musei e anche teatri.

d. Vivo in un paese, è piccolo. Ci sono negozi, però non c'è un cinema.

e. Nel mio paese c'è una farmacia e vivo una stazione dei treni.

f. Cosa c'è nel tuo paese? Nel mio paese c'è una spiaggia bella.

7. Narrow Listening. Gap-fill

a. Vivo _____ una città __________ in Francia. Nel mio__________________

c'è un _________, una _____________ e ___________________. Mi piace

il _____ paese perché è _____________ e bello.

cinema	mio	grande	piscina	paese	tranquillo	in	ristoranti

b. Sono ____________, però vivo in ____________, in un ___________

piccolo. _____________ il mio quartiere perché è ______________, però

______ poco ____________.

vivace	tedesca	quartiere	Amo	rumoroso	un	Spagna

8. Listening Slalom

Listen in Italian and pick the equivalent English words from each column.

e.g. *Nel mio paese c'è un cinema.*

Colour in the boxes for each sentence in a different colour.

a.	In my city there is	because it is big.	swimming pools.
b.	I live in Barcelona.	a gym	There are restaurants and shops.
c.	In my town there are	a cinema,	and a castle.
d.	I love my neighbourhood	there is a beach	and a museum.
e.	I like my town because	shops, but there are not	square, but there isn't a stadium.
f.	In my town there isn't	it is pretty. There is a	but there is a library.

Unit 10. I can say what's in my town: READING

> 1. Read and put the syllables in the cells in the correct order

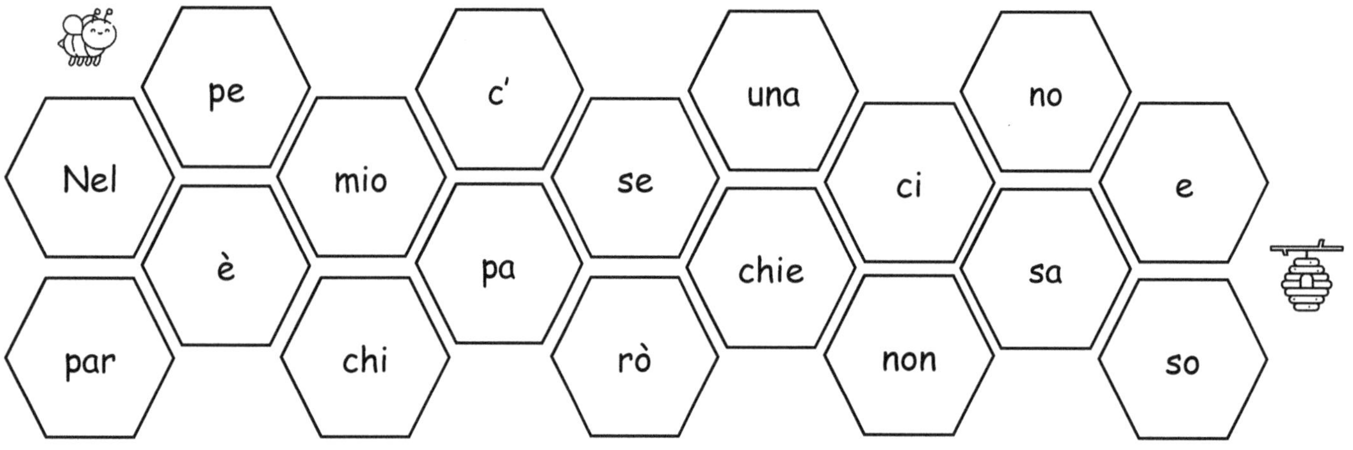

> **a.** In my town there is a church, but there are no parks.
>
> N_____ m_____ p___________ c'è u_____ c____________, p_______
> n_____ c___ s_________ p_____________.

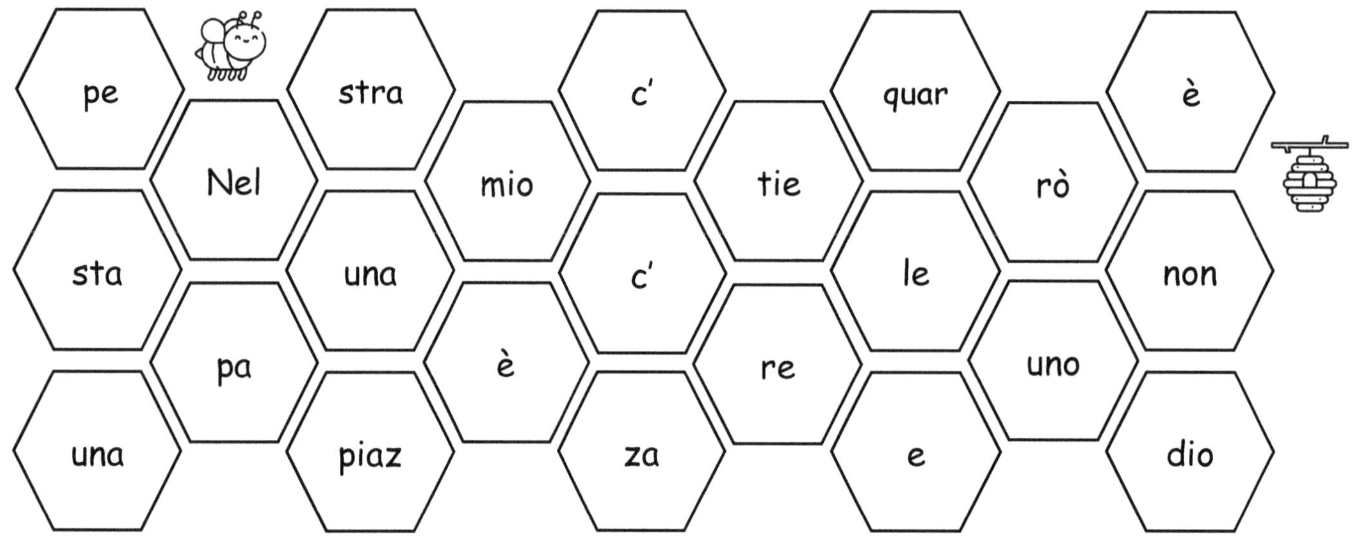

> **b.** In my neighbourhood there is a gym and a square but there isn't a stadium.
>
> N_____ m_____ q___________ c'è u_____ p___________ e u_____
> p_________, p_______ n_______ c'è u_____ s_____________.

THE LANGUAGE GYM

2. True or false
A. Read the paragraphs below and then answer True or False

Ciao, mi chiamo **Giacomo**. Ho undici anni. Vivo a Berlino, la capitale della Germania. Amo la mia città perché è grande e turistica, è anche molto vivace. Nel mio quartiere c'è una libreria, uno stadio e un centro commerciale, però non ci sono cinema.

Ciao, mi chiamo **Sara**. Sono francese, però vivo a Madrid, la capitale della Spagna, normalmente fa caldo in estate. Amo la mia città perché è turistica e bella. Nel mio quartiere c'è una stazione dei treni e un parco, però non ci sono stadi.

	True	False
a. Giacomo is 14 years old.		
b. He doesn't like his city.		
c. His city is small and touristic.		
d. In his neighbourhood there is a stadium.		
e. In his neighbourhood there is a cinema.		
f. Sara is Spanish.		
g. She lives in France.		
h. In Madrid it is normally cold in summer.		
i. In her neighbourhood there is a train station.		
j. In her neighbourhood there are no stadiums.		

B. Find in the texts above the Italian for:

a. The capital of Germany.

b. There is a train station.

c. I love my city.

d. There are no cinemas.

THE LANGUAGE GYM

3. Tick or Cross

A. Read the texts. Tick the box if you find the words in the text, cross it if you do not find them.

- Ciao, mi chiamo **Gisella.**

Ho sette anni. Sono spagnola e vivo in un paese piccolo che si chiama Ronda. Nel mio paese c'è un castello, un museo e una chiesa, però non c'è una stazione dei treni.

- Ciao, mi chiamo **Rosario.**

Ho sei anni. Sono italiano e vivo in una città che si chiama Roma. Mi piace perché è bella. Nel mio quartiere c'è un parco, una libreria e una piscina, però non ci sono cinema.

	✓	✗
a. Ho sette anni.		
b. Sono francese.		
c. Un paese grande.		
d. C'è un castello.		
e. Non ci sono chiese.		
f. Che si chiama.		

g. I am 7 years old.		
h. I am Italian.		
i. Because it is big.		
j. In my neighbourhood.		
k. A swimming pool.		
l. There are no parks.		

B. Find the Italian in the texts above

a. A small town called. _______________________________________

b. There is no train station. _______________________________________

c. I live in a city called Rome. _______________________________________

d. In my neighbourhood there is a park. _______________________________________

e. But there are no cinemas. _______________________________________

4. Language Detective

- Mi chiamo **Mario.** Ho dodici anni. Sono inglese, però vivo a Parigi, la capitale della Francia. A Parigi normalmente c'è bel tempo. Mi piace perché ci sono parchi e cattedrali, e lo stadio del 'Paris Saint-Germain' (PSG).

- Mi chiamo **Roberto.** Ho tredici anni. Sono italiano, però vivo a Madrid, la capitale della Spagna. A Madrid, in estate, fa caldo. Amo la mia città perché è turistica. Ci sono anche musei e lo stadio del Real Madrid.

- Ciao, mi chiamo **Marianna.** Ho undici anni. Sono scozzese, però vivo a Londra, la capitale dell' Inghilterra. A Londra, di solito, piove. Mi piace perché ci sono negozi, però è una città molto rumorosa.

A. Find someone who…

a. …is 13 years old.

b. …lives in England.

c. …lives in a city with museums.

d. …doesn't mention a stadium.

e. …lives in a city with parks.

f. …lives in a noisy city.

g. …is Scottish.

B. Put a cross in the box and underline the corresponding Italian translation. Two are odd.

I am ~~Italian.~~	There are parks.	It usually rains in London.
I love it because it is touristic.	The stadium of PSG	In summer it is warm in Madrid.
But I live in England.	But I live in London	The weather is normally good in Paris.
There are also museums.	I don't like my city	It's a very noisy city.

Unit 10. I can say what's in my town: WRITING

1. Spelling

a. U __ __   s __ __ __ __ __ __ __ __   dei tr __ ni.   A train station.

b. U __ __   s __ __ d __ __.   A stadium.

c. U __ __   p __ __ __ __ __ __ __.   A swimming pool.

d. U __   r __ __ __ __ __ r __ __ t __.   A restaurant.

e. U __ __   b __ b __ __ __ __ t __ __ __.   A library.

f. U __ __   p__ l __ __ t __ __.   A gym.

g. C' __ u __ p __ __ c __.   There is a park.

h. N__ __ c __ s__ __ __ n __ __ __ z__.   There are no shops.

2. Anagrams: unscramble the Italian

a. C'è nu corpa.   *There is a park.*

b. iC noso tretdalica.   *There are cathedrals.*

c. noN ic noso scinepi.   *There are no swimming pools.*

d. iC onso storanriti.   *There are restaurants.*

3. Gapped Translation

a. Nel mio quartiere c'è una palestra e uno stadio.

In my _______________ there is a _______ and a stadium.

b. Nel mio paese c'è una piazza grande.

In my __________ there is a big __________.

c. Vivo a Londra. A Londra ci sono cattedrali e castelli.

I _______ in London. In London _______ are cathedrals and _______.

d. Cosa c'è nel tuo quartiere? C'è una piazza bella.

What ____ there in your neighbourhood? There is a pretty _________.

e. Nella mia città c'è una chiesa e una biblioteca.

In my _______ there is a __________ and a _______________.

4. Split Sentences

a. C'è	**1.** città
b. Nella mia	**2.** mio paese
c. Nel	**3.** piace la mia città
d. Mi	**4.** una stazione dei treni
e. C'è una	**5.** piazza
f. Perchè è	**6.** Francia
g. Vivo in	**7.** bella

a	b	c	d	e	f	g
4						

5. Rock Climbing

Starting from the bottom, pick one chunk from each row to translate the sentences below.

a.	b.	c.	d.	e.
e una cattedrale.	però c'è un supermercato.	ci sono cinema.	e un castello.	e una piscina.
perchè non	una palestra,	una biblioteca	uno stadio	C'è una bella piazza
nel tuo paese?	c'è	non c'è	il mio quartiere	c'è
Nel mio quartiere	Nella mia città	Nel mio paese	Che cosa c'è	Non mi piace

a. In my neighbourhood there is a library and a castle.

____

b. In my city there is a stadium and a cathedral.

____

c. In my town there is not a gym, but there is a supermarket.

____

d. What is there in your town? There is a pretty square and a swimming pool.

____

e. I don't like my neighbourhood because there are no cinemas.

____

6. Fill in the gaps

a. Ciao, mi chiamo Rosario. Ho _________ anni. Sono ____________,

però vivo a Londra. Mi piace perché è molto _________. Nel mio

_________ c'è una ________ e ___ stadio.

grande	italiano	nove	uno	quartiere	piscina

b. Ciao, mi chiamo Nunzia. Sono americana, però _________ a

Maiorca. _____ piace perché _______________ fa caldo. Nella

___ città ______ una chiesa e ci sono_________ piscine.

normalmente	Mi	vivo	C'è	anche	mia

7. Tangled Translation

a. Write the Italian words in English to complete the translation

Hello, **mi chiamo** Anna. **Sono** English, **però** I live **in Italia**. I speak Italian **e tedesco**. In Italy, **normalmente** the **tempo** is good. **Nel mio quartiere** there is **una panetteria** and shops, **però** there is no **stazione dei treni**.

b. Write the English words in Italian to complete the translation

Buongiorno, **my name is** Gianni. Ho **twelve** anni. Vivo **in Germany,** nella capitale che si chiama **Berlin. I like it** perché è **very big** e turistica. **In my** quartiere **there are** una farmacia **and a shop** però non c'è **a bakery**.

Dove vivi **and what** c'è **in your** città?

8. Sentence Puzzle

Put the Italian words in the correct order

a. quartiere Nel mio negozi ci sono anche supermercati. e

In my neighbourhood there are shops and also supermarkets.

b. Cosa tuo paese c'è c'è nel piscina una e piazza. una

What is there in your town? There is a swimming pool and a square.

c. stazioni dei treni. c'è cattedrale, una città però c'è non Nella mia

In my city there is a cathedral, but there are no train stations.

d. bello Il mio paese perché ci ristoranti sono. e negozi è

My town is pretty because there are shops and restaurants.

9. Guided Translation

a. C________, m__ c________ M____________. V________ i_____ u__
c________ b________ c___ s___ c____________ P________.

Hi, my name is Mafalda. I live in a pretty city which is called Paris.

b. V________ i___ u___ c________ b________. N__ m__ c________
c____ s___ n________, p________ n___ c____ s___ p____________.

I live in a pretty city. In my city there are shops, but there are no swimming pools.

c. N__ m__ q________ c____ u____ s__________ e u___ c______,
p________ n___ c____ s___p_____. È m______ n__________.

In my neighbourhood there is a school and a church, but there are no parks. It is very boring.

10. Staircase Translation

Starting from the top, translate each chunk into Italian.
Write the sentences in the grid below.

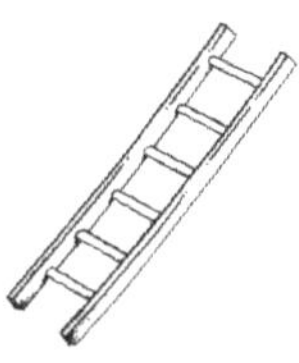

a.	I like	my city.				
b.	I don't like	my town because	there are no cinemas.			
c.	In my neighbourhood	there is a library, but	there are no gyms.	It is pretty.		
d.	In my city	there is a stadium, but	there is no train station.	It is noisy	and also touristic.	
e.	In my town	there is a church, but	there are no cathedrals.	It is small	and also calm,	but it's noisy.

Answers / Risposte

a.	
b.	
c.	
d.	
e.	

 Challenge / Sfida

Can you create 2 more sentences using the words in the staircase grid above?

☆	
☆	

No Snakes No Ladders

PARTENZA	1 Vivo a	2 Vivo a Barcelona	3 Il mio paese	4 La mia città	5 Amo il mio paese	6 Dove vivi?	7 Nel mio quartiere
15 Perché non è brutto	14 È tranquillo	13 È bella	12 Mi piace la mia città perché	11 Ci sono negozi	10 Parchi e ristoranti	9 Non c'è una palestra	8 C'è una piscina
16 Vivo a Londra	17 Il mio paese è rumoroso	18 C'è un super-mercato	19 E una stazione dei treni	20 C'è anche un parco	21 Odio la mia città	22 Il mio paese è piccolo	23 Vivo a Roma
ARRIVO	30 La mia città è vivace	29 Il mio paese è turistico	28 Perché è grande	27 Non mi piace la mia città	26 Non c'è un cinema	25 Un castello e una catedrale	24 C'è una chiesa

No Snakes No Ladders

Unit 9-10

7 In my neighbour-hood	**6** Where do you live?	**5** I love my town	**4** My city	**3** My town	**2** I live in Barcelona
8 There is a swimming pool	**9** There isn't a gym	**10** Parks and restaurants	**11** There are shops	**12** I like my city because	**13** It is pretty (f)
23 I live in Rome	**22** My town is small	**21** I hate my city	**20** There is also a park	**19** And a train station	**18** There is a supermarket
24 There is a church	**25** A castle and a cathedral	**26** There isn't a cinema	**27** I don't like my city	**28** Because it is big	**29** My town is touristic

1 I live in — PARTENZA	**14** It is quiet (m)
15 Because it is not ugly (m) — PARTENZA	
16 I live in London	**17** My town is noisy
30 My city is lively — ARRIVO